Holy Spirit: His Person and Ministry

발행 2017년 1월 20일

지은이 배본철
발행인 윤상문
편집부장 권지현, 김현아
코디네이터 박현수
디자인실장 여수정
디자인 표소영, 박진경
발행처 킹덤북스
등록 제2009-29호(2009년 10월 19일)
주소 경기도 용인시 기흥구 동백동 622-2
문의 전화 031-275-0196 팩스 031-275-0296

ISBN 979-11-5886-084-4 (03230)

Copyright ⓒ 2017 배본철
이 책은 저작권법에 따라 보호받는 저작물이므로 무단전재와 복제를 금지하며,
이 책의 내용의 전부 또는 일부를 이용하려면 반드시 저작권자와 킹덤북스의
서면 동의를 받아야 합니다.

※ 잘못된 책은 구입하신 곳에서 교환하여 드립니다.
※ 책 가격은 표지 뒷면에 있습니다.

킹덤북스(Kingdom Books)는 문서사역을 통해 하나님의 나라를 확장하고,
한국 교회와 세계 교회를 섬기고자 설립된 출판사입니다.

Holy Spirit:
His Person and Ministry

배본철 지음

Rev. Bonjour Bay, Ph. D.
Church History Professor at Sungkyul University, Korea
Representative of Living by Holy Spirit Course
bbc1224@gmail.com

2017

Living by Holy Spirit Course, Headquarters

Preface

Many church leaders and theologians say that the 21st-century must be the period of spirituality for the Christianity. Christian believers will probably consider the necessity and urgency of being powered by the Holy Spirit. However, while there are many talks on spirituality nowaday, people still desperately need and seek the way how to experience and live for the abundant evangelical spirituality.

More than that, there have been a lot of theological controversies on the subject of Holy Spirit, especially in modern Christianity, since the late 19th-century. Various doctrinal and denominational conflicts have made theologians so confused when they come to a theological talk on the subject.

Most of reformed theologians are apt to abstain from talking on spiritual gifts such as speaking in other tongues or prophecies, while the Pentecostals much more focus on the subject than the reformed theologians do. As far as the subject on Spirit Baptism concerned, it has been one of the most controversial issues in theological world.

As a church history professor, and as a researcher on spiritual movements, I've considerably studied the area of Pneumatology for many decades and written not a few books and papers on it. As I looked back to the Pneumatological streams in view of historical perspectives, I could find out the ongoing evangelical core values in them. They brought forth from the 16th century Calvin's Pneumatology and flowed through the 17th, 18th, 19th century and to the 20th-century revival movements and theories.

Union with Christ is one of the most permanent core values of the evangelical Pneumatologies, and others are the *purity* and *power* and *indwelling government of the Spirit of Christ*, etc. Those values will never cease in protestant spiritual movement unless the truth of Gospel disappear. By using the core values, we are able to adjust and harmonize the tendency of misunderstanding and rejection among various theological dispute. Even more over, we are able to find the way of practical power of Holy Spirit by using them.

I've seen the truth that the real power of Holy Spirit mainly springs out from the lifestyle walking humbly with Him. Accordingly, my continuing academic and practical concern has been that 'how can I help the Christian believers and pastors so that they can live life being guided by the Holy Spirit?', and that 'which is the way for the churches and mission fields to bear the abundant fruits of Kingdom harvest by the power of Holy Spirit?'

I have taught and trained pastors, missionaries and lay persons with the practical instruction of Pneumatological resources in many countries. And the ministry, *Living by Holy Spirit Course*, has been expanded worldwidely with the directors and leaders who have been taught through the course.

Holy Spirit: His Person and Ministry is the profound training textbook of the *Living by Holy Spirit Course*. Leaders who finished the course are able to nurture believers with this material, so they can also walk and minister with the Holy Spirit. More than that, the leaders also make another leaders who are equipped with the ability that can nurse others as well.

This book is not just only for the delivery of the Pneumatological knowledge, but also for the training for the practical abound fruitions. The book has 12 lessons and 52 sections in it. The composition is good to train lay people for 52 weeks, or, more intensively, for 12 weeks so that they can be certificated as leaders after finishing the course. 3 or 4 days and nights intensive leader course will be quite available for the pastors or missionaries who are already well-equipped in the area.

Holy Spirit: His Person and Ministry has some apparent characteristics that differentiate it from other books on the subject of Pneumatology.

Firstly, everyone will easily understand the complicated streams and difficult ideas of Pneumatology through the careful reading of the book.

Secondly, the book is useful not just only for the training course, but also for all men and women who lead cell group meeting or Bible study.

Thirdly, the book is so inter-denominational and evangelical that every Christian can freely use this without any doctrinal doubt or conflict.

Lastly, readers will be guided day after day to the lifestyle walking with the Holy Spirit and to the ministry being empowered by Him.

This is my earnest prayer for all the readers; May the Lord sanctify and strengthen you so that the grace of Christlikeness and the power of evangelism will be overflown to your lives. And may the Lord give peace to you all who devote your lives to expand the Kingdom of God on the earth, Amen.

Jan. 1, 2017

Bonjour Bay

Contents

Preface   5

Lesson 1
The Triune God and the Holy Spirit   13

1. Creation and the Holy Spirit 15 / 2. Relationship of Triune God 20 / 3. The Spirit of Jesus Christ 25 / 4. The Ministry of Holy Spirit 30

Lesson 2
Holy Spirit and the Regeneration   37

1. Human Spirit and the Holy Spirit 39 / 2. Ministry that makes Repentance 44 / 3. Personal Indwelling of the Holy Spirit 49 / 4. Spiritual Guidance 54

Lesson 3
Fruit of the Holy Spirit   61

1. Union with Christ 63 / 2. Fruit and Sanctification of the Holy Spirit 67 / 3. Personal Government of the Holy Spirit 72 / 4. Christlikeness 76

Lesson 4
Holy Spirit and Sanctification   83

1. Sin and Sanctification 85 / 2. Death of Old Being 90 / 3. Full Consecration 96 / 4. Law of the Holy Spirit of Life 101

Lesson 5
Fullness of the Holy Spirit   109

1. Definition of Fullness of the Holy Spirit 111 / 2. Purpose of Fullness of the Holy Spirit 116 / 3. The Way of Fullness of the Holy Spirit 120 / 4. The Way of Continual Fullness of the Holy Spirit 124

Lesson 6
Baptism with the Holy Spirit   131

1. Definition of Spirit Baptism 133 / 2. Types of Reformed-line Spirit Baptism 136 / 3. Types of Wesleyan-line and of Charismatic-line Spirit Baptism 139 / 4. Dual Dimension of Spirit Baptism 142 / 5. Power of Spirit Baptism 147

Lesson 7
Manifestation of the Holy Spirit and the Power   155

1. Power of the Holy Spirit and Evangelism 157 / 2. Manifestation of the Holy Spirit(I) 163 / 3. Manifestation of the Holy Spirit(II) 171 / 4. Holy Spirit and Glossolalia 189

Lesson 8
Holy Spirit and the Healing   197

1. Holy Spirit and the Holistic Healing 199 / 2. Inner Healing 204 / 3. Holy Spirit and Dream 208 / 4. Physical Healing 214 / 5. Holy Spirit and Evil Spirits 218

Contents

Lesson 9
Pneumatology and the Radical Spiritual Movement   225

1. Various Types of the Radical Spiritual Movements 227 / 2. Radical Syncretic Spirituality 231 / 3. Radical Renewal Spirituality 235 / 4. Radical schismatic Spirituality 239

Lesson 10
Streams of the Protestant Spiritual Movement   245

1. Calvin's Pneumatology 247 / 2. Puritan Pneumatology 252 / 3. Wesley's Spiritual Movement 256 / 4. Spiritual Movement of the 19th Century United States 260 / 5. Modern Charismatic Christianity 265

Lesson 11
Holy Spirit and the Communities   273

1. Communities of New Birth 275 / 2. Communities of Healing and Restoration 279 / 3. Communities being guided by the Holy Spirit 282 / 4. Communities of Full Dedication 286 / 5. Communities of the Lordship of Holy Spirit 290

Lesson 12
The Lordship of Holy Spirit   295

1. Developmental Course of the Pneumatology 297 / 2. Holistic Pneumatology 301 / 3. Definition of the Lordship of Holy Spirit 305 / 4. Life of the Lordship of Holy Spirit 309

Appendix I: The Main Points in Church History   316

Appendix II: Rise of the Protestant Pneumatology   318

Appendix III: The Power of Holy Spirit Seminar   320

Appendix IV: The Lordship of Holy Spirit   326

Lesson 1

The Triune God and the Holy Spirit

Creation and the Holy Spirit

1. Holy Spirit has worked since the Creation of the world.

• Our God is the triune God; God the Father, Son Jesus Christ and the Holy Spirit.

• When God created the heavens and the earth, then was the Holy Spirit as well.

[Gen. 1:1-2] (1)In the beginning God created the heavens and the earth. (2)Now the earth was formless and empty, darkness was over the surface of the deep, and the Spirit of God was hovering over the waters.

• Some say that the Holy Spirit is only working in us, while God the Father once worked for the creation of the world, and while

Jesus only for redemptive ministry before. But the theory can't be true. On the contrary, we rather to say that the three persons worked before and even now work together and they are in unison. No person of Trinity can be separated from each other.

2. Holy Spirit is working for the new creation in human being.

• Holy Spirit worked before not just only for the creation of the world but also is working for the new creation of human being.

[2 Cor. 1:21-22] (21) Now it is God who makes both us and you stand firm in Christ. He anointed us, (22) set his seal of ownership on us, and put his Spirit in our hearts as a deposit, guaranteeing what is to come.

• It is the Holy Spirit who makes us repent our sins, and also the same Holy Spirit who regenerates and sanctifies us.

3. Holy Spirit restores the Lost Paradise anew.

• All men have lost their glorious blessing of Garden of Eden which God bestowed, since Adam and Eve committed sin against God there.

• But God the Father prepared the way of restoration for the lost souls by sending His Son to the world.

• This Son bore our all sins and took them to the cross, and He died for our sins.

> [Isaiah 53:5-6] (5) But he was pierced for our transgressions, he was crushed for our iniquities; the punishment that brought us peace was upon him, and by his wounds we are healed. (6) We all, like sheep, have gone astray, each of us has turned to his own way; and the LORD has laid on him the iniquity of us all.

• Therefore, whoever receives Jesus' grace into his heart will be saved from all his past sins and will have eternal life.
• Holy Spirit will come and live in us, for He is the Spirit of Jesus Christ.
• Holy Spirit performs the mighty works in us, which is, more than over, the redemptive ministry of God. By doing that, He restores the Kingdom of God in us. The Kingdom of God in us is the real existence of fullness of righteousness, peace and joy in the Holy Spirit.

> [Rom. 14:17] For the kingdom of God is not a matter of eating and drinking, but of righteousness, peace and joy in the Holy Spirit.

• Regarding the righteousness in Spirit, now you are able to seek

His Kingdom and righteousness rather than your own selfish desires.

• As for the peace, God will give you abundant peace wherever you go and whatever you do as far as you live in accordance with His Spirit.

• Joy of the Lord will fill your heart overflowingly as you seek His face earnestly without ceasing.

❦ Questions for the Spiritual Ministry

1. What is the scripture evidence of the existence of Holy Spirit at the creation of the world?

_____

2. How does the Holy Spirit work for the new creation of human being?

_____

3. Could you explain the whole process of Paradise Lost and Paradise Restored throughout your life?

_____

✝ *Prayers of Daily Application*

1. Thank God for His guiding your life; your past, present and even your future.

2. Pray for your full dedication to God so that the Holy Spirit will change and sanctify your soul day by day.

Relationship of Triune God

1. Danger of Dynamistic Monarchianism

• The Bible clearly says that there is only one God, and that three persons are in one in God.

> [John 14:16-17] (16)And I will ask the Father, and he will give you another Counselor to be with you forever-- (17)the Spirit of truth. The world cannot accept him, because it neither sees him nor knows him. But you know him, for he lives with you and will be in you.

• I will - Jesus , He will - Father, another Counselor - Holy Spirit
• There are some false teachings on Triune God, and the one of them is the teaching that Jesus was not true God. The teaching

says that Jesus was only a human being in His early years, and later He became God.

• Likewise, nowadays, some people say that Jesus was only a human not God. They neither accept Jesus' redemption nor confess their sins to Jesus.

• However, the Bible declares that Jesus was and is God Himself as well as a perfect human being.

2. Danger of Modalistic Monarchianism

• Another false teaching says that Jesus was not a human but God only. In the ancient Christian times, the Gnostics believed that there is a dualistic world in which the contradiction exists such as light and darkness, spirit and flesh, good and evil, etc. They believed that if Jesus was God who really forgave sins, He should not be a physical being, for all the material and physical were sinful according to their conviction. They said, therefore, Jesus must be absolutely spiritual rather than physical.

[1 John 4:1-3] (1) Dear friends, do not believe every spirit, but test the spirits to see whether they are from God, because many false prophets have gone out into the world. (2) This is how you can recognize the Spirit of God: Every spirit that acknowledges that Jesus Christ has come in the flesh is from God, (3) but every spirit

that does not acknowledge Jesus is not from God. This is the spirit of the antichrist, which you have heard is coming and even now is already in the world.

• Such belief is not biblical. Because, the Bible Clearly says that Jesus is truly a human being as well as true God.

3. Danger of Subordinate Trinity

• The last false theory on Trinity is the teaching that Father God is the first, and the next is Jesus Christ, and the last is the Holy Spirit. In other words, Father God is the biggest, and Jesus Christ is bigger than the Holy Spirit. And the Holy Spirit is the smallest. This is a false teaching.

• If we recognize the Holy Spirit as the lowest God in Trinity, we shall fall into a very dangerous thought that the Holy Spirit is nothing but the power or influence of God which has no personality. See below;

[Eph. 4:30] And do not grieve the Holy Spirit of God, with whom you were sealed for the day of redemption.

• Bible says there is a perfect harmony and unity in Triune God. Accordingly, they worked together and help and exhort one another in perfect unison.

🞂 Questions for the Spiritual Ministry

1. What is the Dynamistic Monarchianism? Why is this theory dangerous in Christian faith?

_____

2. Why is Gnosticism the model of Modalistic Monarchianism? Enumerate the characters of it.

_____

3. Suppose that someone's belief is based on the theory of Subordinate Trinity, what will he speak about the status of Holy Spirit?

_____

✝ Prayers of Daily Application

1. Ask Holy Spirit that He could examine your heart whether you are in the right belief of Trinity God.

2. Pray that you determine to serve the Holy Spirit as the almighty personal God who has intelligence, emotion and free will.

The Spirit of Jesus Christ

1. Holy Spirit is the Spirit of Jesus Christ as well as of God.

• Jesus said that the Counselor would come to you.

[John 14:25-26] (25)All this I have spoken while still with you. (26) But the Counselor, the Holy Spirit, whom the Father will send in my name, will teach you all things and will remind you of everything I have said to you.

• The Counselor means *Parakletos*, the person who is with us and counsels for us. It also means the teacher who gives grace and takes care of us. All these expressions show us that the Holy Spirit is the person who really wants to have close fellowship with you.

[John 16:7] But I tell you the truth: It is for your good that I am going away. Unless I go away, the Counselor will not come to you; but if I go, I will send him to you.

- Jesus was the real counselor of the disciples when he lived on the earth. But Jesus said, "It is for your good that I am going away," for if he would go away, he said, he would send the Holy Spirit to them.

[John 14:16] And I will ask the Father, and he will give you another Counselor to be with you forever.

- Another counselor; Jesus was the counselor for them at that time, but the Holy Spirit will be another counselor for us today.
- Jesus was within the limits of the sphere of time and space when he was on the land. But now the freedom has come to Him, for He is no more within the limits of the sphere of time and space. He exists in Spirit.
- We should regard the Holy Spirit as Jesus Himself and revere Him, for the Holy Spirit is the Spirit of Jesus Christ.

2. Receiving Jesus is the same experience with receiving the Holy Spirit.

• Some say that receiving Jesus is different experience from receiving the Holy Spirit. But that is the wrong belief. If that was true, we would believe in many gods; God Jesus and God the Spirit. By no means!

[John 7:37-39] (37) On the last and greatest day of the Feast, Jesus stood and said in a loud voice, "If anyone is thirsty, let him come to me and drink. (38) Whoever believes in me, as the Scripture has said, streams of living water will flow from within him." (39) By this he meant the Spirit, whom those who believed in him were later to receive. Up to that time the Spirit had not been given, since Jesus had not yet been glorified.

• Receiving Jesus is same as receiving the Holy Spirit, and when you are filled with the mind of Jesus, then is the time for you to be filled with the Holy Spirit.

3. The more we experience the Holy Spirit, the more we are able to know Jesus.

• There are some false teachings on the Holy Spirit nowaday.
• Since the Holy Spirit is the Spirit of Jesus, the more we

experience the Holy Spirit, the more we are able to know Jesus.

[Rom. 8:9] You, however, are controlled not by the sinful nature but by the Spirit, if the Spirit of God lives in you. And if anyone does not have the Spirit of Christ, he does not belong to Christ.

Questions for the Spiritual Ministry

1. What was the real meaning of Jesus saying, "It is for your good that I am going away"?

_____

2. Explain why receiving Jesus is the same experience with receiving the Holy Spirit.

_____

3. Why do we become like Jesus more as we more experience the Holy Spirit?

_____

✝ *Prayers of Daily Application*

1. Ask yourself whether you are serving the Holy Spirit as if you see Jesus Christ face to face. And pray for your closer relationship with Him.

2. Intercede for the wrong or misguided spiritual groups around you so that they could turn back from the false belief on Holy Spirit.

The Ministry of Holy Spirit

1. Holy Spirit makes us realize our sins.

• Holy Spirit convicts the world of guilt; that is, the Holy Spirit convicts our souls, since human souls have been ruined as the world of guilt.

> [John 16:7-8] (7) But I tell you the truth: It is for your good that I am going away. Unless I go away, the Counselor will not come to you; but if I go, I will send him to you. (8) When he comes, he will convict the world of guilt in regard to sin and righteousness and judgment:

• What does the Holy Spirit convict? In Regard to sin and righteousness and judgement.

- Regarding to sin; not believing in Jesus is sin.
- Regarding to righteousness; only receiving Jesus' grace is righteousness.
- Regarding to judgement; there will be no other way to escape from final judgement except relying on Jesus who will be your attorney at the judgement day.
- Through the repentance ministry of Holy Spirit, you are able to access Jesus who is your salvation day after day.

2. Holy Spirit leads us to the experience of the Union with Christ.

- Holy Spirit is the mediator between God and men.
- Holy Spirit, especially, applies Jesus' redemptive work to you.
- Since the Holy Spirit is the spirit, He transcends time and space, and applies Jesus' death and resurrection to your lives.

[John 15:3-5] (3) You are already clean because of the word I have spoken to you. (4) Remain in me, and I will remain in you. No branch can bear fruit by itself; it must remain in the vine. Neither can you bear fruit unless you remain in me. (5) "I am the vine; you are the branches. If a man remains in me and I in him, he will bear much fruit; apart from me you can do nothing."

• So in Spirit, you are united with Jesus' death as well as with His resurrection. This is the truth of Union with Christ.

3. Holy Spirit sanctifies us.

• Holy Spirit is the Spirit of holiness. He gives you strength to pursue the way of holiness.

• The more you have deep relationship with the Holy Spirit, the more you resemble Jesus.

[Eph. 4:13] until we all reach unity in the faith and in the knowledge of the Son of God and become mature, attaining to the whole measure of the fullness of Christ.

• The purpose of your holiness is attaining to the whole measure of fullness of Christ.

♥ Questions for the Spiritual Ministry

1. Explain the meaning of in regard to sin and righteousness and judgement.

2. What is your experience of Union with Christ? How does the Holy Spirit work for it in you?

_____

3. Describe what will be your lifelong process of holiness through the ministry of Holy Spirit.

_____

✝ *Prayers of Daily Application*

1. Ask Holy Spirit that He would search and reveal your inner motive whether there might be a certain sinfulness that grieves God.

2. To believe in Jesus is to live with the solid confession that you are united with Jesus in His crucifixion and resurrection. Confess that even today!

NOTE

NOTE

NOTE

Lesson 2

Holy Spirit and the Regeneration

01

Human Spirit and the Holy Spirit

1. God created the human spirit.

• God made human being according to His image. What will be the meaning of God's image?

[Gen. 1:26-27] (26) Then God said, "Let us make man in our image, in our likeness, and let them rule over the fish of the sea and the birds of the air, over the livestock, over all the earth, and over all the creatures that move along the ground." (27) So God created man in his own image, in the image of God he created him; male and female he created them.

• In our image; Why our image not my image? That plural pronoun might be an expression that denotes the truth of Triune

God.

- Men was created by God who is Spirit, that's why we need to worship Him in spirit.

> [John 4:24] God is spirit, and his worshipers must worship in spirit and in truth.

- In order to worship God in spirit and in truth, you should devote yourself to worship Him with all your heart.
- All people have their own spirit that can be aware of the existence of God, and such perception in human heart came from God.

> [Rom. 1:19-20] (19) since what may be known about God is plain to them, because God has made it plain to them. (20) For since the creation of the world God's invisible qualities--his eternal power and divine nature--have been clearly seen, being understood from what has been made, so that men are without excuse.

- However, non-Christian do not accept God as their king and Lord because of their stubborn pride and sinfulness.
- Those who do not accept God as their Lord won't be able to get their salvation at the judgement day.

2. The original function of human spirit is to seek God.

• Human soul once had the function that could make fellowship with God very closely, but the function has been ruined since Adam's fall.

> [1 Cor. 2:12-14] (12) We have not received the spirit of the world but the Spirit who is from God, that we may understand what God has freely given us. (13) This is what we speak, not in words taught us by human wisdom but in words taught by the Spirit, expressing spiritual truths in spiritual words. (14) The man without the Spirit does not accept the things that come from the Spirit of God, for they are foolishness to him, and he cannot understand them, because they are spiritually discerned.

• Your spirit can be restored when you receive Jesus into your heart as your Lord.

> [Acts 23:1] Paul looked straight at the Sanhedrin and said, "My brothers, I have fulfilled my duty to God in all good conscience to this day."

• Good conscience means good spirit, that is, the regenerated spirit.

• Then, you are able to serve God with your conscience which has been restored by God's grace.

3. Holy Spirit restores the original function of human spirit.

• Holy Spirit gives you the real conviction that you are God's children.

[Rom. 8:16] The Spirit himself testifies with our spirit that we are God's children.

• Holy Spirit speaks to your spirit the way of truth.

[John 16:13] But when he, the Spirit of truth, comes, he will guide you into all truth. He will not speak on his own; he will speak only what he hears, and he will tell you what is yet to come.

Questions for the Spiritual Ministry

1. Non-believers don't accept Christ as their savior, even though in them there is a spirit that God made. Why not?

---

2. Why did the human spirit lose the function of fellowship with God?

_____

3. What's the meaning of that Holy Spirit testifies?

_____

† *Prayers of Daily Application*

1. Pray for the purity of your conscience so that you can be guided by the Holy Spirit with blameless heart.

2. Pray that you would not be disobedient to the Holy Spirit who always wants to lead you the way of truth.

Ministry that makes Repentance

1. **Holy Spirit makes you repent your sin that does not believe in Jesus.**

• People think that the sin is nothing more than the matter of ethic or moral.

[Isa. 59:1-3] (1) Surely the arm of the LORD is not too short to save, nor his ear too dull to hear. (2) But your iniquities have separated you from your God; your sins have hidden his face from you, so that he will not hear. (3) For your hands are stained with blood, your fingers with guilt. Your lips have spoken lies, and your tongue mutters wicked things.

• But the Lord looks at the heart more than the outward behavior.

[John 16:9] in regard to sin, because men do not believe in me;

- Sin is, more than over, not believing in Jesus Christ as savior.

[Rom. 1:21] For although they knew God, they neither glorified him as God nor gave thanks to him, but their thinking became futile and their foolish hearts were darkened.

- People already knew the existence of God. However, they neither glorify God nor give thanks to Him.

[John 16:8] When he comes, he will convict the world of guilt in regard to sin and righteousness and judgment:

- The real repentance is, therefore, turning back their life to God by the influence of Holy Spirit.
- When the Holy Spirit inspires you, first of all, He convicts you your sin.
- Holy Spirit, then, assures you the truth that only Jesus is the righteousness of God.
- Holy Spirit also makes you realize the existence of final judgement.
- By the ministry of Holy Spirit, you are able to repent your sins

and to know Jesus as your righteousness and to be aware of the final judgement of God. Then you are able to come to Jesus.

2. Holy Spirit makes you repent every sins that you committed.

- Even though you are born-again Christians, it is true that you sometimes commit sins.

> [1 John 3:9] No one who is born of God will continue to sin, because God's seed remains in him; he cannot go on sinning, because he has been born of God.

- Actually, born-again Christians have a motive in heart that wills to do God's will.
- But there still be a sinful desire in their heart.
- The battle ground in heart between God's desire and sinful desire.
- When you are tempted by evil desire, you commit sin to God.
- You can be forgiven whenever you confess your sins to God.

3. Holy Spirit makes you repent to be wholly dedicated to God.

• Every born-again Christian has a root of sinfulness that makes him sin, which is the inheritance that came from Adam. We call this Original Sin.

> [Rom. 14:23] But the man who has doubts is condemned if he eats, because his eating is not from faith; and everything that does not come from faith is sin.

• Original Sin should be eradicated.
• Holy Spirit makes you repent to be wholly dedicated to God.

> [2 Cor. 10:5] We demolish arguments and every pretension that sets itself up against the knowledge of God, and we take captive every thought to make it obedient to Christ.

• As you commit yourselves to God without ceasing, you are able to live a holy life.

✐ Questions for the Spiritual Ministry

1. Describe the dimensions of the repentance ministry of Holy Spirit in human being.

_____

2. What's the basis of the forgiveness of sins as we repent of them?

_____

3. Could you define the meaning of Original Sin? What's the difference between Original Sin and actual sins?

_____

† *Prayers of Daily Application*

1. Ask the Holy Spirit that He would remind you of your secret depravities or faults that you've forgot.
2. Let the Holy Spirit make you gladly submit to the Lord's will in every deed and speech.

Personal Indwelling of the Holy Spirit

1. **Holy Spirit works for you to be regenerated.**

• You are able to know that the Spirit of Jesus knocks at the door of your heart in order that He comes into your lives.

[Rev. 3:20] Here I am! I stand at the door and knock. If anyone hears my voice and opens the door, I will come in and eat with him, and he with me.

• Regeneration, that is, new birth, takes place when the Spirit of Christ comes into your heart and dwells in your lives.

[John 14:17] the Spirit of truth. The world cannot accept him, because it neither sees him nor knows him. But you know him, for *he lives with you and will be in you.*

• Indeed, the Spirit of Truth, the Holy Spirit, lives with you and in you.

[2 Cor. 5:17] Therefore, if anyone is in Christ, he is a new creation; the old has gone, the new has come!

• And you and I are living in the Holy Spirit, that is, we are living in the Spirit of Christ.
• Just as Christ was dead to sin, so you are already dead to sin in Christ, for you are in the body of Christ. Just as Jesus Christ was alive to God the Father, so you are to live toward God. This is the new life in Christ.

2. Holy Spirit himself wants to dwell in the heart of the regenerated man personally.

• God really wants you hold fast to Him.

[Josh. 23:8] But you are to hold fast to the LORD your God, as you have until now.

• Enoch walked with God throughout his whole life, and God

really appreciated his faithfulness.

[Gen. 5:24] Enoch walked with God; then he was no more, because God took him away.

• The first thing you need to do in serving God is to walk with Him gladly in every moment.

[Eph. 4:30] And do not grieve the Holy Spirit of God, with whom you were sealed for the day of redemption.

3. Holy Spirit dwells in you in order to accomplish the goal of your sanctification.

[Eph. 4:13] until we all reach unity in the faith and in the knowledge of the Son of God and become mature, attaining to the whole measure of the fullness of Christ.

• The more you know God, the more you grow up in your spirituality, attaining to the whole measure of the fullness of Christ.

[John 14:20] On that day you will realize that I am in my Father, and you are in me, and I am in you.

- Holy Spirit works in you to make you all one in Christ, sharing the unity and love of God.

  [Gal. 4:19] My dear children, for whom I am again in the pains of childbirth until Christ is formed in you.

- This should be the ultimate goal of your born-again life, even your Christlikeness.

Questions for the Spiritual Ministry

1. What's the meaning of new being or new creature in Christ?

   _____

2. Describe the meaning of personal indwelling of the Holy Spirit in believers.

   _____

3. What's the ultimate goal of the indwelling of Holy Spirit in you?

   _____

✝ *Prayers of Daily Application*

1. Today, have you lived well in accordance with the Holy Spirit? Ask God's help for your closer intimacy with the Holy Spirit.

2. Christlikeness is the will of God for those who are in Christ Jesus. Pray that all your deeds, speeches and motives are weighed and nurtured by the Holy Spirit so that you become grow more and more like Christ.

Spiritual Guidance

1. There may be many misunderstandings around you in regard of the teaching of Spiritual guidance.

• The Bible expressed that the young Samuel heard the God's voice.

[1 Sam. 3:8-9] (8) The LORD called Samuel a third time, and Samuel got up and went to Eli and said, "Here I am; you called me." Then Eli realized that the LORD was calling the boy. (9) So Eli told Samuel, "Go and lie down, and if he calls you, say, 'Speak, LORD, for your servant is listening.'" So Samuel went and lay down in his place.

• Some enthusiastic Christians use the expression *I heard God's voice.*

[John 14:25-26] (25)"All this I have spoken while still with you. (26)But the Counselor, the Holy Spirit, whom the Father will send in my name, will teach you all things and will remind you of everything I have said to you."

• Such expression frequently raises many misunderstandings in Christian societies.

[John 16:13] But when he, the Spirit of truth, comes, he will guide you into all truth. He will not speak on his own; he will speak only what he hears, and he will tell you what is yet to come.

• What does this passage mean in regard of the Spiritual guidance?
• What does the term *revelation* theologically mean? Does God bestow the special revelation to every Christian nowaday?

2. What is Spiritual guidance?

• Hearing God's voice does not mean that God always talk to you just as human talk to each other by using their natural voice.
• You'd better use the expression *I am following the God's guidance* rather than *I hear God's voice*.

[Gal. 5:18] But if you are led by the Spirit, you are not under law.

• The guidance of Spirit always works in your life, even in your prayer time, during your conversation, and in your worship time.
• When you begin to realize the will of God in your heart, then is the time you are guided by the Holy Spirit. That could be said that you heard the voice of God.
• You'd better to say, *I was guided by the Holy Spirit* rather than *I heard the voice of God*.

3. How can you live to be guided by the Holy Spirit?
• Holy Spirit gives you His guidance by using your native inner function rather than by using the extraordinary way of expression.
• If your emotion submit to the Lord, it will be used as the wonderful tool of Holy Spirit. So your free will and intelligence as well.

[2 Cor. 10:5] We demolish arguments and every pretension that sets itself up against the knowledge of God, and we take captive every thought to make it obedient to Christ.

• You should examine your experiences, testifying them whether they are from the Holy Spirit or not. The experience that comes from the Holy Spirit must require a minimum these two conditions;

- Firstly, they should be biblical.
- Secondly, they must be fit to your conscience.

❦ Questions for the Spiritual Ministry

1. Talk about the misguided belief of spiritual guidance such as *I heard the God's voice*.

_____

2. Share the practical examples of spiritual guidance in your daily lives.

_____

3. What are the two steps how we examine whether the experience come from the Holy Spirit?

_____

✝ Prayers of Daily Application

1. Pray that not to be inclined to the sinful nature but be aware of the guidance of Holy Spirit at all times.

2. Is there any sphere of your life that always fail to follow Spiritual guidance? Pray that the Holy Spirit triumphs over the sphere with His absolute sovereignty.

NOTE

NOTE

Lesson 3

Fruit of the Holy Spirit

Union with Christ

1. **Having faith in Jesus means to live a life that is unified with Jesus Christ.**

• Because of His love for you, Jesus came into your souls through the mediate work of Holy Spirit.

[John 15:5-7] (5) I am the vine; you are the branches. If a man remains in me and I in him, he will bear much fruit; apart from me you can do nothing. (6) If anyone does not remain in me, he is like a branch that is thrown away and withers; such branches are picked up, thrown into the fire and burned. (7) If you remain in me and my words remain in you, ask whatever you wish, and it will be given you.

- Jesus who lives in you really wants to live and share His life with you.
- Because of His sacrificial love, Jesus remains in you, and you can also remain in Him; the glory of Union with Christ.

2. To believe 'Union with Christ' should be the secret of the empowered Christian life.

- Union with Christ is based on the truth that you are dead with Jesus and now you live with Jesus. In His crucifixion, you have been dead on the cross. Likewise, in His resurrection, you are living toward God.

> [Gal. 2:20] I have been crucified with Christ and I no longer live, but Christ lives in me. The life I live in the body, I live by faith in the Son of God, who loved me and gave himself for me.

- To apply Union with Christ is the top secret of the overcoming Christian life.

3. The teaching of 'Union with Christ' is one of the most important factor of the evangelical Spiritual movement.

- There are lots of strange and non-biblical teachings nowaday.

You need to be very much cautious about them.

[Rom. 6:3-5] (3) Or don't you know that all of us who were baptized into Christ Jesus were baptized into his death? (4) We were therefore buried with him through baptism into death in order that, just as Christ was raised from the dead through the glory of the Father, we too may live a new life. (5) If we have been united with him like this in his death, we will certainly also be united with him in his resurrection.

• The sound Biblical teaching of Holy Spirit always sets its focus on the doctrine of Union with Christ.

❦ Questions for the Spiritual Ministry

1. Explain the life of Union with Christ, citing the illustration of John 15:5-7.

_____

2. How do we live a victorious life in accordance with the belief of Union with Christ?

_____

3. Apply and confess Rom. 6:3-5 in the viewpoint of overcoming victorious life.

―――――――――――――――――――――――――――――

✝ *Prayers of Daily Application*

1. Keep in mind that the spiritual truth of Union with Christ be with you always in everywhere.

2. Declare and pray that the tremendous power of Jesus' crucifixion and resurrection will be manifested in your daily lives.

Fruit and Sanctification of the Holy Spirit

1. Christian should not gratify the sinful desires.

• There are two principles conflicting each other in your souls.

> [Gal. 5:16-18] (16)So I say, live by the Spirit, and you will not gratify the desires of the sinful nature. (17)For the sinful nature desires what is contrary to the Spirit, and the Spirit what is contrary to the sinful nature. They are in conflict with each other, so that you do not do what you want. (18)But if you are led by the Spirit, you are not under law.

• If you follow the sinful desire, you will commit sins. On the contrary, if you are led by the Holy Spirit, you will bear good fruit of the Spirit.

[Rom. 6:6] For we know that our old self was crucified with him so that the body of sin might be done away with, that we should no longer be slaves to sin.

• You should not gratify the sinful desire in our heart, for you know that you are already dead to sin on the Cross with Jesus.

2. Christian should live a life filled with Spiritual fruit by the guidance of Holy Spirit.

• If you are led by the Holy Spirit, the fruit of Spirit grows up in your lives.

[Gal. 5:22-24] (22)But the fruit of the Spirit is love, joy, peace, patience, kindness, goodness, faithfulness, (23)gentleness and self-control. Against such things there is no law. (24)Those who belong to Christ Jesus have crucified the sinful nature with its passions and desires.

• The fruit of Holy Spirit is the personality or character of Jesus Christ who is in you as Spirit. Because Jesus is full of love, joy, peace, patience, kindness, goodness, faithfulness, gentleness and self-control.

3. Christian should imitate Jesus Christ day by day through the life overflown with Spiritual fruit.

[Gal. 5:16-26] (16) So I say, live by the Spirit, and you will not gratify the desires of the sinful nature. (17) For the sinful nature desires what is contrary to the Spirit, and the Spirit what is contrary to the sinful nature. They are in conflict with each other, so that you do not do what you want. (18) But if you are led by the Spirit, you are not under law. (19) The acts of the sinful nature are obvious: sexual immorality, impurity and debauchery; (20) idolatry and witchcraft; hatred, discord, jealousy, fits of rage, selfish ambition, dissensions, factions (21) and envy; drunkenness, orgies, and the like. I warn you, as I did before, that those who live like this will no t inherit the kingdom of God. (22) But the fruit of the Spirit is love, joy, peace, patience, kindness, goodness, faithfulness, (23) gentleness and self-control. Against such things there is no law. (24) Those who belong to Christ Jesus have crucified the sinful nature with its passions and desires. (25) Since we live by the Spirit, let us keep in step with the Spirit. (26) Let us not become conceited, provoking and envying each other.

- All these verses take the present tense; live(16), are led(18), live(25), keep in step with(25).
- That means that living by Spirit must be the continuing practice

in your daily lives rather than an extraordinary or instantaneous experience.

[2 Cor. 4:16] Therefore we do not lose heart. Though outwardly we are wasting away, yet inwardly we are being renewed day by day.

• Only try to follow His guidance every day, then you will bear much fruit and become a persons like Jesus.

Questions for the Spiritual Ministry

1. How do the two principles conflict each other in your souls?

_____

2. Do you know why the word *fruit* in *fruit of the Holy Spirit* only take singular number?

_____

3. Let's talk about the lifestyle of walking with the Holy Spirit daily.

_____

† *Prayers of Daily Application*

1. Pray that you may not to be enticed to the sinful temptation but to be led by the Holy Spirit.

2. Pray everyday for imitating Christ, bearing abundant Spiritual fruit.

Personal Government of the Holy Spirit

1. **How can you live the life filled with the Holy Spirit continuously?**

• Some are filled with joy and peace that come from their faith, yet others may be not.

[Phil. 4:4] *Rejoice in the Lord always. I will say it again: Rejoice!*

• Why not? Because of lack of faith? Or sins? Or God does not love us? No! Absolutely not!

• God really wants you to be filled with great joy of the Lord and with the fullness of Spirit. Then, how can you abide with these graces?

2. What reliable witness will be given to you when the Holy Spirit govern you personally?

• When the Holy Spirit controls you, He gives you an accurate sign of His government. That sign is apparently seen in the major functions of your soul; emotion, intelligence and free will.

• 1 Thess. 5:16-18 denotes you the profitable guideline that you can follow the life being filled with the Spirit without ceasing.

[1 Thess. 5:16-18] (16)Be joyful always; (17)pray continually; (18) give thanks in all circumstances, for this is God's will for you in Christ Jesus.

• Be joyful always (in the Lord)!
• Pray continually (with the Lord)!
• Give thanks in all circumstances (to the Lord)!

[2 Cor. 10:5] We demolish arguments and every pretension that sets itself up against the knowledge of God, and we take captive every thought to make it obedient to Christ.

3. What preparation must be needed when you want to live the lives controlled by the Holy Spirit?

• How can you discriminate whether you are controlled by the

Holy Spirit?

• Examine yourselves how much you are filled with joy, prayer and thanks because of the Lord. That examination must be the remarkable sign of your soul whether you are filled with the Spirit or not.

> [James 4:8] Come near to God and he will come near to you. Wash your hands, you sinners, and purify your hearts, you double-minded.

• So yield yourselves humbly to God and just practice this truth along with your emotion, intelligence and free will. Then you are able to enjoy the Spirit-filled lives day after day.

Questions for the Spiritual Ministry

1. Do you know why only few of us can live a Spirit-filled life continuously?

_____

2. Explain 1 Thess. 5:16-18 in the viewpoint of Spiritual fullness. How can you examine yourself whether you are full of Spirit by

using these verses?

___

3. Ask yourself whether you are controlled by the Holy Spirit in your every deed, speech and motive.

___

† Prayers of Daily Application

1. Let your intelligence, emotion and free will be subjected to personal government of Holy Spirit today.
2. Pray that you could obey the Word of God; be joyful always, pray without ceasing, and give thanks in all circumstances.

Christlikeness

1. Do you understand that believing in Jesus is the life guided by the Holy Spirit?

[Mark 1:16-18] (16) As Jesus walked beside the Sea of Galilee, he saw Simon and his brother Andrew casting a net into the lake, for they were fishermen. (17) "Come, follow me," Jesus said, "and I will make you fishers of men." (18) At once they left their nets and followed him.

[Matt. 9:9] As Jesus went on from there, he saw a man named Matthew sitting at the tax collector's booth. "Follow me," he told him, and Matthew got up and followed him.

• Dietrich Bonhoeffer who was one of the well-known theologians in Germany during the world war II. In his saying, Bonhoeffer clearly differentiated costly grace from costless grace. Costless grace is, he said, the dangerous enemy of the church, forgiveness without repentance, and baptism without education. It is the closing door to Christ rather than the open door.

• But the costly grace is, he said, like the treasure hidden in the field. It is the sincere faith to follow after the shepherd's voice. When Jesus called Matthew, he stood soon and followed Jesus. When Jesus called Simon and his brother Andrew, they left the net and followed Him. That is like the costly grace.

[Rom. 8:14] because those who are led by the Spirit of God are sons of God.

• Jesus Christ lives in you as Spirit. When you follow the Holy Spirit earnestly at all times, you are able to follow Jesus in His Spirit as well. This is the lifestyle of costly grace.

2. What should you do in order to live the lives guided by the Spiritual guidance?

[Luke 14:26-27] (26) If anyone comes to me and does not hate his *father and mother, his wife and children, his brothers and sisters-- yes, even his own life--he cannot be my disciple. (27)And anyone who does not carry his cross and follow me cannot be my disciple.*

- First of all, you should deny yourselves and your all things for Jesus' sake. That is the necessary condition of Jesus' disciples.

[Matt. 16:24-25] (24)Then Jesus said to his disciples, "If anyone would come after me, he must deny himself and take up his cross and follow me. (25)For whoever wants to save his life will lose it, but whoever loses his life for me will find it."

- And take up your cross everyday.
- Whoever dares to bear his cross, he can really enjoy the power of resurrection through the guidance of Holy Spirit.

3. What kind of power will be revealed to those who live in accordance with the Spiritual guidance?

- They will probably bear much fruit, which is, the fruit of Holy Spirit.

[Gal. 5:22-23] (22)But the fruit of the Spirit is love, joy, peace, patience, kindness, goodness, faithfulness, (23)gentleness and self-

control. Against such things there is no law.

- They will pursue the goal of Christlikeness throughout their lifetime.

[Eph. 4:13] until we all reach unity in the faith and in the knowledge of the Son of God and become mature, attaining to the whole measure of the fullness of Christ.

[Eph. 4:15] Instead, speaking the truth in love, we will in all things grow up into him who is the Head, that is, Christ.

Questions for the Spiritual Ministry

1. Distinguish costly grace from costless grace.

_____

2. What are the necessary conditions of discipleship of Christ?

_____

3. Are you trying to be a man of perfume of Christ whether in your deed or speech?

_____

† Prayers of Daily Application

1. Have you lived today as Costly Grace or as Costless Grace? If you have more lived of Costless Grace, confess your unawareness and infirmity of your soul to Jesus.

2. Are you willing to sacrifice yourself to Jesus as disciple, following His way without wavering?

NOTE

NOTE

Lesson 4

Holy Spirit and Sanctification

Sin and Sanctification

1. Fullness of the Holy Spirit brings you the grace of sanctification that can triumph over the sinfulness.

[1 Thess. 4:3] It is God's will that you should be sanctified: that you should avoid sexual immorality.

• Our God wants you to be holy men of God, since God is your father and you are His children. Therefore, just as your God is holy, so you should be holy..

[Eph. 5:18] Do not get drunk on wine, which leads to debauchery. Instead, be filled with the Spirit.

- Here, *be filled with the Spirit* in this sentence takes a passive voice grammatically, and is the same expression with *be controlled by the Spirit* or *be guided by the Spirit*.
- That is to say, Spirit-filled life is the life being guided and controlled by the Holy Spirit at all times.

> *[1 Cor. 12:8-11] (8) To one there is given through the Spirit the message of wisdom, to another the message of knowledge by means of the same Spirit, (9) to another faith by the same Spirit, to another gifts of healing by that one Spirit, (10) to another miraculous powers, to another prophecy, to another distinguishing between spirits, to another speaking in different kinds of tongues, and to still another the interpretation of tongues. (11) All these are the work of one and the same Spirit, and he gives them to each one, just as he determines.*

> *[Gal. 5:22-23] (22) But the fruit of the Spirit is love, joy, peace, patience, kindness, goodness, faithfulness, (23) gentleness and self-control. Against such things there is no law.*

2. In order to be filled with the Holy Spirit, you must submit to the Lord with your own free will.

- You should be watchful and prayerful, for you are apt to lose the fullness of Spirit even though you already experienced it.

• Why then does God allow you to lose the fullness of Spirit so quickly? To know the reason, you will need to ponder on Adam and Eve in the garden of Eden.

[Gen. 3:24] *After he drove the man out, he placed on the east side of the Garden of Eden cherubim and a flaming sword flashing back and forth to guard the way to the tree of life.*

• Adam and Eve misused their free will that God gave them.
• Probably you will be in just same condition as Adam.

3. You can defeat the sinful temptations as you rejoice in the accomplished victory that the Lord made.

• Deliverance from Sin is quite possible for you!

[Rom. 6:6] *For we know that our old self was crucified with him so that the body of sin might be done away with, that we should no longer be slaves to sin.*

• What is the source of human pride?

[Gen. 3:1-6] *(1)Now the serpent was more crafty than any of the wild animals the LORD God had made. He said to the woman, "Did God really say, 'You must not eat from any tree in the garden'?" (2) The woman said to the serpent, "We may eat fruit from the trees in the garden, (3) but God did say, 'You must not eat fruit from the tree that is in the middle of the garden, and you must not touch it, or you will die.'" (4) "You will not surely die," the serpent said to the woman. (5) "For God knows that when you eat of it your eyes will be opened, and you will be like God, knowing good and evil." (6) When the woman saw that the fruit of the tree was good for food and pleasing to the eye, and also desirable for gaining wisdom, she took some and ate it. She also gave some to her husband, who was with her, and he ate it.*

• Weakness, infirmities, errors or ignorance are quite different from wilful sinning.

Questions for the Spiritual Ministry

1. Could you briefly explain the definition of the fullness of Holy Spirit?

_____

2. Is your free will always obedient to the guidance of Holy Spirit?

_____

3. By using Rom. 6:6, describe how you can enjoy the overcoming life that always prevail over temptations.

_____

✝ *Prayers of Daily Application*

1. Make your free will always be obedient to the guidance of Holy Spirit.

2. Apply the truth that Jesus has accomplished on the cross to you so that you could sufficiently defeat the temptation of sinning.

Death of Old Being

1. **You are to know the truth that your old being has been dead with Christ Jesus on the cross.**

[Rom. 6:3-5] (3) Or don't you know that all of us who were baptized into Christ Jesus were baptized into his death? (4) We were therefore buried with him through baptism into death in order that, just as Christ was raised from the dead through the glory of the Father, we too may live a new life. (5) If we have been united with him like this in his death, we will certainly also be united with him in his resurrection.

• Thorough the chapter Rom. 6, you are able to realize the relationship between Jesus and yourself.

- Jesus lived on the earth in the 1st century, yet you are living in the 21st century. Jesus once lived in Israel, meanwhile everyone of you is living in each different country. Most of you might have never been in Israel, and there is now no one in this world who ever lived in the 1st century.
- When Jesus was dead on the cross, you were also dead with Him on the cross. When Jesus was resurrected from death, you were also risen from death. How will it be possible?

> [1 Cor. 12:13] *For we were all baptized by one Spirit into one body--whether Jews or Greeks, slave or free--and we were all given the one Spirit to drink.*

- Not by power nor by might. Which is only possible by the mediative ministry of Holy Spirit. What a glorious mediation of the Holy Spirit it is! That is very important notion as we try to understand this wonderful and mysterious secret which is in Christ.
- Holy Spirit always transcends the sphere of time and space within which the human beings are always confined.
- Holy Spirit was there when Jesus was crucified on the cross, and was there when Jesus was risen from the dead and ascended to heaven, for the Holy Spirit is the Spirit of God and of Jesus Christ. God the Father and the Son Jesus Christ and the Holy Spirit is one in unity. Each person never act anything apart without the mutual

communication among each other.

• The same Spirit who acted in Jesus' death 2,000 years ago also acts for you now, applying all the truth and power of crucifixion with Christ as the mediator between Jesus and you. The same Spirit who acted in Jesus' resurrection 2,000 years ago also strengthens you today, applying the power of Jesus' resurrection.

2. When you believe and confess the truth that your sinful body has been destroyed, you are able to defeat the sinful temptations.

[Rom. 6:6-10] (6) For we know that our old self was crucified with him so that the body of sin might be done away with, that we should no longer be slaves to sin-- (7) because anyone who has died has been freed from sin. (8) Now if we died with Christ, we believe that we will also live with him. (9) For we know that since Christ was raised from the dead, he cannot die again; death no longer has mastery over him. (10) The death he died, he died to sin once for all; but the life he lives, he lives to God.

• Verse 6 clearly says that it was not your ego but your old being that was crucified with Jesus on the cross. Your ego, yourself, must exist as long as you live. You'll never see the world without perceiving the existence of yourself. But, as for the old being in you, that must be eradicated.

• Old being means the previous sinful or egoistic lifestyle you have had before, which is the lifestyle when you were out of Christ.

[Rom. 6:11] *In the same way, count yourselves dead to sin but alive to God in Christ Jesus.*

• So you need to confess and declare the truth that Jesus prepared for you. When you believe and stand firm in that truth, you are able to defeat all kinds of temptations you face with.

3. If you dedicate your body to God and use it for the righteous weapon to God, you can overcome any sins.

[Rom. 6:12-13] *(12) Therefore do not let sin reign in your mortal body so that you obey its evil desires. (13) Do not offer the parts of your body to sin, as instruments of wickedness, but rather offer yourselves to God, as those who have been brought from death to life; and offer the parts of your body to him as instruments of righteousness.*

• We can see 3 important nouns in verses 12 and 13; yourselves, sin and body.

- Self is you, yourself.
- Sin is not yourself, even though it may act in you. Sin is sin itself not yourself.
- Body is originally neutral, neither good nor bad. When body is inclined to sin, it will be sinful. When it is inspired by God, it will be holy.
- Therefore, you, Christians, must declare that your body is not yours but God's, and that it does not belong to sin but to God. You will need such proclamation for your fully consecrated life to God.

❦ Questions for the Spiritual Ministry

1. Explain how the born-again Christians were crucified with Jesus Christ.

_____

2. Do you confess the truth *crucifixion with Jesus* whenever you are tempted?

_____

3. Can you boldly confess that your body is not for yourself but only for God?

_____

✝ Prayers of Daily Application

1. Meditate the truth your old being has been already dead, and declare it today!
2. Yield your body and self to God as the powerful weapons of God!

Full Consecration

1. Full consecration is that you dedicate your body as a living sacrifice to God.

[1 Cor. 6:19-20] (19)Do you not know that your body is a temple of the Holy Spirit, who is in you, whom you have received from God? You are not your own; (20)you were bought at a price. Therefore honor God with your body.

• Your body was a tool of Sin when you were sinner, yet now it became temple of God. Holy Spirit of God lives in you.

[Rom. 8:9] You, however, are controlled not by the sinful nature but by the Spirit, if the Spirit of God lives in you. And if anyone *does not have the Spirit of Christ, he does not belong to Christ.*

[Rom. 6:13] Do not offer the parts of your body to sin, as instruments of wickedness, but rather offer yourselves to God, as those who have been brought from death to life; and offer the parts of your body to him as instruments of righteousness.

• Just as Jesus offered His body to God, so you should dedicate your body as a living sacrifice to God.

[Phil. 1:20-21] (20)I eagerly expect and hope that I will in no way be ashamed, but will have sufficient courage so that now as always Christ will be exalted in my body, whether by life or by death. (21) For to me, to live is Christ and to die is gain.

[Rom. 12:1] Therefore, I urge you, brothers, in view of God's mercy, to offer your bodies as living sacrifices, holy and pleasing to God--this is your spiritual act of worship.

• While the sacrifice of Old Testament was the dead sacrifice, that of New Testament is the living sacrifice.
• In this verse, spiritual act of worship means the reasonable worship, that is to say, full consecration begins at the reasonable worship which offers your body to God.

2. Full consecration is that you are controlled by the power of Holy Spirit throughout the function of your intelligence, emotion and free will.

[Rom. 12:2] Do not conform any longer to the pattern of this world, but be transformed by the renewing of your mind. Then you will be able to test and approve what God's will is--his good, pleasing and perfect will.

• In order to be controlled by the Holy Spirit, you first need to be transformed by the renewing of your mind.

[2 Cor. 10:5] We demolish arguments and every pretension that sets itself up against the knowledge of God, and we take captive every thought to make it obedient to Christ.

• You will need to take captive every thought to make it obedient to Christ at all times.

[1 Thess. 5:16-18] (16)Be joyful always; (17)pray continually; (18) give thanks in all circumstances, for this is God's will for you in Christ Jesus.

• As you continually practice these words, you are effectively able to be trained by the Holy Spirit daily.

3. Full consecration by which you are able to discriminate the will of God in every circumstances.

[Rom. 12:2] Do not conform any longer to the pattern of this world, but be transformed by the renewing of your mind. Then you will be able to test and approve what God's will is--his good, pleasing and perfect will.

• The real consecration is, negatively, that not conforming any longer to the pattern of this world, and positively, that being transformed by the renewing of your mind.
• Christian is, in biblical point of view, the person who does not follow the pattern of this world, rather, who pursues the way of the renewal of mind.

❧ Questions for the Spiritual Ministry

1. Contrast the New Testament sacrifice with the Old Testament sacrifice. What's the living sacrifice?

_____

2. What do you need to prepare for your fully dedicated life to God?

_____

3. What are the negative and positive attitudes of the real consecration?

_____

✝ Prayers of Daily Application

1. Examine yourself whether you are consecrated by God, and if not, repent any sphere of yourself which is not yet ruled by the Holy Spirit.

2. Pray that the Holy Spirit can always rule over your intelligence, emotion and free will.

Law of the Holy Spirit of Life

1. Anyone who is in Christ must be the person who lives in accordance with the Holy Spirit.

[Rom. 8:1-4] (1) Therefore, there is now no condemnation for those who are in Christ Jesus, (2) because through Christ Jesus the law of the Spirit of life set me free from the law of sin and death. (3) For what the law was powerless to do in that it was weakened by the sinful nature, God did by sending his own Son in the likeness of sinful man to be a sin offering. And so he condemned sin in sinful man, (4) in order that the righteous requirements of the law might be fully met in us, who do not live according to the sinful nature but according to the Spirit.

- Verse 1, those who are in Christ Jesus; They do not live according to the sinful nature but according to the Spirit(4).
- There is no condemnation to them. Why not? Because through Christ Jesus the law of Spirit of life set them free from the law of sin and death(2).

2. There is a distinct difference between the one who follows the flesh and the one who lives in the Holy Spirit.

[Rom. 8:5-11] (5) Those who live according to the sinful nature have their minds set on what that nature desires; but those who live in accordance with the Spirit have their minds set on what the Spirit desires. (6) The mind of sinful man is death, but the mind controlled by the Spirit is life and peace; (7) the sinful mind is hostile to God. It does not submit to God's law, nor can it do so. (8) Those controlled by the sinful nature cannot please God. (9) You, however, are controlled not by the sinful nature but by the Spirit, if the Spirit of God lives in you. And if anyone does not have the Spirit of Christ, he does not belong to Christ. (10) But if Christ is in you, your body is dead because of sin, yet your spirit is alive because of righteousness. (11) And if the Spirit of him who raised Jesus from the dead is living in you, he who raised Christ from the dead will also give life to your mortal bodies through his Spirit, who lives in you.

- There may be two kinds of Christians; One is the man who lives according to the sinful nature. The other is the one who lives in accordance with the Spirit.
- Think about the former; It is no doubt that he is a Christian, yet he always has his mind set on what the nature desires(5).
- The mind of him is death(6).
- His mind is hostile to God(7).
- His mind does not submit to God(7).
- He cannot please God(8).
- What about, then, the latter? He is also a Christian, and his lifestyle is quite different from the former.
- He belongs to Christ(9).
- His body is dead because of sin, yet his spirit is alive because of righteousness(10).
- Jesus Christ will give eternal life to him through His Spirit(11).

3. Whoever being filled with the Holy Spirit also meets the tribulations as well as the glorious victory.

- The uppermost goal of your spiritual life is the life being controlled by Spirit at all times.

[Rom. 8:12-17] (12)Therefore, brothers, we have an obligation--but it is not to the sinful nature, to live according to it. (13)For if *you live according to the sinful nature, you will die; but if by the Spirit you put to death the misdeeds of the body, you will live, (14) because those who are led by the Spirit of God are sons of God. (15) For you did not receive a spirit that makes you a slave again to fear, but you received the Spirit of sonship. And by him we cry, "Abba, Father." (16) The Spirit himself testifies with our spirit that we are God's children. (17) Now if we are children, then we are heirs--heirs of God and co-heirs with Christ, if indeed we share in his sufferings in order that we may also share in his glory.*

- It is not the life subjected by sinful nature but by the Holy Spirit(12).
- If you are led by the Spirit, you can put to death the misdeed of your body(13).
- Then, you are Sons of God(14). Because you received the Spirit of sonship(15). So you can cry Abba Father(15).
- The Spirit testifies that you are God's children(16).
- You are heirs of God. You will share in His sufferings in order that you may also share in His glory(17).

❡ Questions for the Spiritual Ministry

1. Considering Rom 8:1-4, what kinds of person do you think of real Christians like?

_____

2. Clearly distinguish the person who are led by the Holy Spirit from sinful man.

_____

3. Do you fully understand why God permit trials even to those who are filled with the Holy Spirit?

_____

✝ *Prayers of Daily Application*

1. Pray for not following the sinful desire, instead, for being led by the guidance of Holy Spirit.
2. Pray that you would gladly pursue the way of tribulation which Jesus Christ had walked.

NOTE

→ NOTE

Lesson 5

Fullness of the Holy Spirit

Definition of Fullness of the Holy Spirit

1. It is called as 'Fullness of the Holy Spirit' when someone's soul is filled with the Spirit of Jesus Christ.

[Deut. 6:4-5] (4)Hear, O Israel: The LORD our God, the LORD is one. (5)Love the LORD your God with all your heart and with all your soul and with all your strength.

• Being filled with the Holy Spirit is to be filled with the Spirit of Christ, for the Holy Spirit is the Spirit of Christ.
• Jesus Christ began to live in you as soon as you accepted Him as your Savior. But He cannot fully control your heart yet because of the inherited sinfulness in you; doubt, unbelief, arrogancy, worldliness, etc.

• When you are full of the Holy Spirit, you can live a Christ-centered life just like the apostle Paul admonished like below:

> [Eph. 5:18-21] (18) Do not get drunk on wine, which leads to debauchery. Instead, be filled with the Spirit. (19) Speak to one another with psalms, hymns and spiritual songs. Sing and make music in your heart to the Lord, (20) always giving thanks to God the Father for everything, in the name of our Lord Jesus Christ. (21) Submit to one another out of reverence for Christ.

2. It is called as 'Fullness of the Holy Spirit' when someone submits to Christ wholeheartedly.

• Some say they are already filled with the Holy Spirit, yet, to tell the truth, some of them might not be true.

• Examine yourself whether you are obedient to the Lord at all times and in everything.

• Repent your sins so you can be restored, if you are not yet fully submit to the Lord. Then you can be filled with the Spirit again.

> [James 4:8] Come near to God and he will come near to you. Wash your hands, you sinners, and purify your hearts, you double-minded.

3. It is called as 'Fullness of the Holy Spirit' when someone associates with the Holy Spirit intimately.

• Spirit Fullness; it is walking with the Lord very closely.

• In the garden of Eden, God really wanted to make close relationship with Adam and Eve.

• However, men disobeyed God and were afraid of God accordingly. Adam hid himself from God's presence. That can be called as the state of Paradise Lost.

[Gen. 3:8-10] (8) Then the man and his wife heard the sound of the LORD God as he was walking in the garden in the cool of the day, and they hid from the LORD God among the trees of the garden. (9) But the LORD God called to the man, "Where are you?" (10) He answered, "I heard you in the garden, and I was afraid because I was naked; so I hid."

• Jesus Christ came to your life and shook hands with you, so you can be restored from the broken relationship with God.

[Rev. 3:20] Here I am! I stand at the door and knock. If anyone hears my voice and opens the door, I will come in and eat with him, and he with me.

• Jesus is life-giver for your Paradise Restored.

• Let's try to live a holy life that God pleases with.

❦ Questions for the Spiritual Ministry

1. By using Eph. 5:18-21, check up the characteristics of fullness of the Holy Spirit.

_____

2. Why submission to Christ is essential for us to be filled with the Spirit?

_____

3. Do you have a close intimacy with the Holy Spirit everyday?

_____

† *Prayers of Daily Application*

1. Be alert and pray at all times so that you can obey God's will in accordance with the Holy Spirit.

2. Make every effort to have the close intimacy with the Holy Spirit.

Purpose of Fullness of the Holy Spirit

1. **You are able to imitate Christ more and more by living a life being filled with the Holy Spirit.**

• You should be holy, for the Lord your God the Father is holy.

[Lev. 11:44-45] (44)I am the LORD your God; consecrate yourselves and be holy, because I am holy. Do not make yourselves unclean by any creature that moves about on the ground. (45) I am the LORD who brought you up out of Egypt to be your God; therefore be holy, because I am holy.

• Why do you call the Spirit of God as the Holy Spirit? Because the Holy Spirit is the Spirit of holiness.

• What's the meaning of holiness? Holiness is, briefly saying, to become like Jesus Christ.

[Eph. 4:13] until we all reach unity in the faith and in the knowledge of the Son of God and become mature, attaining to the whole measure of the fullness of Christ.

2. You receive the power of purity in heart by being filled with the Holy Spirit.

[Matt. 3:11] I baptize you with water for repentance. But after me will come one who is more powerful than I, whose sandals I am not fit to carry. He will baptize you with the Holy Spirit and with fire.

• When the Holy Spirit fills your heart, He cleanses your heart with His consuming fire, the fire of purification. Then all the sinful affections in your heart can be eradicated by the fire.

[Psalm 51:10-11] (10) Create in me a pure heart, O God, and renew a steadfast spirit within me. (11) Do not cast me from your presence or take your Holy Spirit from me.

• Did you receive the fire of purification? Have you cleansed from all impurities and wrong affections in heart?

- Ask the Lord so He can purify your heart with His sanctifying power.

3. You receive the power for service by being filled with the Holy Spirit.

- Have you received this power from on high?

[Luke 24:48-49] (48) You are witnesses of these things. (49) I am going to send you what my Father has promised; but stay in the city until you have been clothed with power from on high.

[Acts 1:8] But you will receive power when the Holy Spirit comes on you; and you will be my witnesses in Jerusalem, and in all Judea and Samaria, and to the ends of the earth.

- Luke said, "until you have been clothed with power from on high." And in Acts, "You will receive power."
- This power is the power for Christian service.
- Why don't you ask the Lord, so He can pour His heavenly power upon you?

❦ Questions for the Spiritual Ministry

1. What do you think about the ultimate goal of the born-again Christian life?

___

2. How can you describe the purity of heart by the power of Holy Spirit?

___

3. Talk about the various phases of power for service by the Holy Spirit.

___

† *Prayers of Daily Application*

1. Try to be filled with the Holy Spirit whatever you do so that you can sufficiently fulfill all the tasks God has entrusted.

2. Cast all your burdens to the Lord in order that your heart could be stilled by God's overflowing peace.

The Way of Fullness of the Holy Spirit

1. **You can experience the Fullness of the Holy Spirit by the petition of repentance with faith.**

- What is the meaning of repentance?

[Psalm 51:1-4] (1)For the director of music. A psalm of David. When the prophet Nathan came to him after David had committed adultery with Bathsheba. Have mercy on me, O God, according to your unfailing love; according to your great compassion blot out my transgressions. (2)Wash away all my iniquity and cleanse me from my sin. (3)For I know my transgressions, and my sin is always before me. (4)Against you, you only, have I sinned and done what is evil in your sight, so that you are proved right when you speak and justified when you judge.

- the deeper repentance of believers

[1 John 1:8-9] (8) If we claim to be without sin, we deceive ourselves and the truth is not in us. (9) If we confess our sins, he is faithful and just and will forgive us our sins and purify us from all unrighteousness.

- The deeper you repent to God, the more you can be filled with the Holy Spirit.

[Luke 11:13] If you then, though you are evil, know how to give good gifts to your children, how much more will your Father in heaven give the Holy Spirit to those who ask him!

[Acts 8:15-17] (15) When they arrived, they prayed for them that they might receive the Holy Spirit, (16) because the Holy Spirit had not yet come upon any of them; they had simply been baptized into the name of the Lord Jesus. (17) Then Peter and John placed their hands on them, and they received the Holy Spirit.

2. You can experience the Fullness of Holy Spirit through the sincere worship and praise.

[Exodus 40:34-35] (34) Then the cloud covered the Tent of Meeting, and the glory of the LORD filled the tabernacle. (35) Moses could not enter the Tent of Meeting because the cloud had settled upon it, and the glory of the LORD filled the tabernacle.

- Tabernacle in the Old Testament times
- worship in spirit and in truth
- Our God is the God who is in our praise.
- Be ready to receive the fullness of Holy Spirit!

3. You can experience the Fullness of Holy Spirit when you receive the Word of God wholeheartedly.

[Acts 10:44] While Peter was still speaking these words, the Holy Spirit came on all who heard the message.

- You will need to read, memorize and meditate the Word of God daily.

❧ Questions for the Spiritual Ministry

1. Why do you need the repentance even after you are being regenerated?

_____

2. What attitude do you need to be filled with the Holy Spirit during your worship time?

_____

3. Talk about the examples you received the fullness of Holy Spirit when you read and meditated the Bible or listened the sermon.

_____

✝ *Prayers of Daily Application*

1. Prepare your heart to be filled with the Holy Spirit as you sing psalms and spiritual songs and as you worship the Lord with all your heart.

2. Expect that you could be filled with the Holy Spirit while you are listening the sermon.

The Way of Continual Fullness of the Holy Spirit

1. You should always approach the means of grace as possible as you can.

[Exodus 40:36-38] (36)In all the travels of the Israelites, whenever the cloud lifted from above the tabernacle, they would set out; (37) but if the cloud did not lift, they did not set out--until the day it lifted. (38)So the cloud of the LORD was over the tabernacle by day, and fire was in the cloud by night, in the sight of all the house of Israel during all their travels.

[1 Thess. 5:19] Do not put out the Spirit's fire.

• Worship is the best way to near God.

- Prayer is the dialogue with God.
- Bible meditation
- Service
- Counseling
- The Church gives you a lot of means of grace.

2. You are to walk with the Lord everyday continuously.

> [1 Thess. 5:16-18] (16)Be joyful always; (17)pray continually; (18) give thanks in all circumstances, for this is God's will for you in Christ Jesus.

- Joy, prayer and thanksgiving are the apparent characters of being filled with Spirit.

> [Eph. 6:12] For our struggle is not against flesh and blood, but against the rulers, against the authorities, against the powers of this dark world and against the spiritual forces of evil in the heavenly realms.

- You, Christian, have spiritual warfare to fight against the demonic power.

3. You are to live for the ideal of imitating Christ throughout your lifetime.

• Your lifestyle should be changed in order to have a victorious spiritual life.

> [Col. 3:2-3] (2)Set your minds on things above, not on earthly things. (3)For you died, and your life is now hidden with Christ in God.

• Think about the things above, and do not think about the earthly things.

> [Col. 1:28] We proclaim him, admonishing and teaching everyone with all wisdom, so that we may present everyone perfect in Christ.

• Your life-goal is to become like Christ Jesus.

✐ Questions for the Spiritual Ministry

1. Enumerate the means of grace you have experienced.

_____

2. To walk with the Lord without ceasing, what are you going to make up your mind?

___

3. Whom do you need to resemble as Jesus' disciple?

___

† *Prayers of Daily Application*

1. Examine yourself today whether you live in the means of grace.
2. Repent and pray more for your deeper spirituality, even for becoming like Christ.

NOTE

NOTE

NOTE

Lesson 6

Baptism with the Holy Spirit

01

Definition of Spirit Baptism

1. **There is an interpretation that the time of Spirit Baptism is simultaneous with the time of Regeneration.**

• Two different explanations of Spirit Baptism

[1 Cor. 12:12-13] (12) The body is a unit, though it is made up of many parts; and though all its parts are many, they form one body. So it is with Christ. (13) For we were all baptized by one Spirit into one body--whether Jews or Greeks, slave or free--and we were all given the one Spirit to drink.

2. **There is an interpretation that the time of Spirit Baptism is differ from the time of Regeneration.**

- Baptism also means *immersion* or *being filled*.

[Acts 2:1-4] (1) When the day of Pentecost came, they were all together in one place. (2) Suddenly a sound like the blowing of a violent wind came from heaven and filled the whole house where they were sitting. (3) They saw what seemed to be tongues of fire that separated and came to rest on each of them. (4) All of them were filled with the Holy Spirit and began to speak in other tongues as the Spirit enabled them.

- Many of Wesleyan or Pentecostal denominations generally follow such explanation.

3. You need to focus on the power of Spirit Baptism rather than the matter of time of it.
- One of the hottest issues of Pneumatological controversy today
- We need to deal with the matter of power of Spirit Baptism more than of the time of it.

[1 Cor. 4:19-20] (19) But I will come to you very soon, if the Lord is willing, and then I will find out not only how these arrogant people are talking, but what power they have. (20) For the kingdom of God is not a matter of talk but of power.

❦ Questions for the Spiritual Ministry

1. Could you explain two different doctrinal notions of Spirit Baptism?

_____

2. Why do many of Wesleyan and Pentecostals believe that the time of Spirit Baptism is differ from the time of regeneration?

_____

3. What examples of the power of Spirit Baptism have you seen in the Bible?

_____

† *Prayers of Daily Application*

1. You will need spiritual power for your overcoming Christian life. Ask God it now!

2. Let the Holy Spirit bestow His mighty power upon you, and you will be able to perform God's task with His power.

Types of Reformed-line Spirit Baptism

1. Regeneration=Spirit Baptism, after that, fullness of the Holy Spirit

[Rom. 8:9] You, however, are controlled not by the sinful nature but by the Spirit, if the Spirit of God lives in you. And if anyone does not have the Spirit of Christ, he does not belong to Christ.

- Abraham Kuiper, Richard B. Gaffin, John Stott, Bill Bright, Billy Graham
- This is the line of Orthodox Reformed Pneumatology.

2. Spirit Baptism as the power for service

[Luke 24:48-49] (48)You are witnesses of these things. (49)I am going to send you what my Father has promised; but stay in the city until you have been clothed with power from on high."

- Dwight L. Moody, Reuben A. Torrey, Charles G. Finney
- One of the characteristics of Reformed Spiritual Movement

3. Spirit Baptism as the Christ' perfect control

[1 Cor. 3:16] Don't you know that you yourselves are God's temple and that God's Spirit lives in you?

- William E. Boardman, Andrew Murray, Albert B. Simpson
- Another characteristic of Reformed Spiritual Movement

❧ Questions for the Spiritual Ministry

1. How do the theologians of Orthodox Reformed Pneumatology explain about Spirit Baptism?

2. What is the emphasis of Spirit Baptism theory of the Reformed Spiritual leaders such persons as D. L. Moody or R. A. Torrey?

___

3. Describe the meaning of Spirit Baptism as Christ' perfect control.

___

† *Prayers of Daily Application*

1. Ask God that He would bestow the heavenly power upon you so that you can proclaim gospel with spiritual power.

2. Have you ever experienced the Spirit Baptism as Christ' perfect control over you? If not, prepare yourself so that the Holy Spirit would reign on you.

Types of Wesleyan-line and of Charismatic-line Spirit Baptism

1. Spirit Baptism as the purity and power

[Psalms 51:10] Create in me a pure heart, O God, and renew a steadfast spirit within me.

[Ezekiel 36:26-27] (26)I will give you a new heart and put a new spirit in you; I will remove from you your heart of stone and give you a heart of flesh. (27)And I will put my Spirit in you and move you to follow my decrees and be careful to keep my laws.

- John Wesley, George D. Watson, Phoebe Palmer
- Traditional holiness view of Wesleyan Pneumatology

2. Spirit Baptism that accompanies speaking in other tongues

[Acts 10:44-46] (44) While Peter was still speaking these words, the Holy Spirit came on all who heard the message. (45) The circumcised believers who had come with Peter were astonished that the gift of the Holy Spirit had been poured out even on the Gentiles. (46) For they heard them speaking in tongues and praising God.

• Charles F. Parham, William J. Seymour, John L. Sherill, Francis MacNutt
• Classical Pentecostal Pneumatology & many of Charismatic Renewal follow the line.

3. Regeneration, after that, Spirit Baptism accompanying charismatic fullness of the Holy Spirit

• John Wimber, Peter Wagner, Charles H. Craft, Benny Hynn
• Vineyard Movement and the most of the Third Wavers

[1 Cor.12:1] Now about spiritual gifts, brothers, I do not want you to be ignorant.

❡ Questions for the Spiritual Ministry

1. What is the type of Wesleyan-line Spirit Baptism?

_____

2. What sign of Spirit Baptism does the Classical Pentecostal Pneumatology emphasize?

_____

3. Who are the representatives of Vineyard movement and of the Third Wave?

_____

✝ Prayers of Daily Application

1. Pant for the Spirit Baptism as the purity and power, and experience it today!

2. Pray that the manifestation and gifts of Holy Spirit would be overflown in your ministry.

Dual Dimension of Spirit Baptism

1. Spirit Baptism: Dimension of Spiritual Truth

- Union with Christ

[Rom. 6:1-10] (1)What shall we say, then? Shall we go on sinning so that grace may increase? (2)By no means! We died to sin; how can we live in it any longer? (3)Or don't you know that all of us who were baptized into Christ Jesus were baptized into his death? (4)We were therefore buried with him through baptism into death in order that, just as Christ was raised from the dead through the glory of the Father, we too may live a new life. (5)If we have been united with him like this in his death, we will certainly also be united with him in his resurrection. (6)For we know that our old self was crucified with him so that the body of sin might be done away with, that we should no longer be slaves to sin--(7) because anyone who has died has been freed from sin. (8) Now if we died with Christ, we believe that we will also live with him. (9) For we know that since Christ was raised from the dead, he cannot die again; death no longer has mastery over him. (10) The death he died, he died to sin once for all; but the life he lives, he lives to God.

- Contrast between the meaning of Spirit Baptism and of Water Baptism

[1 Cor. 12:13] (13) For we were all baptized by one Spirit into one body--whether Jews or Greeks, slave or free--and we were all given the one Spirit to drink.

2. Spirit Baptism: Dimension of Experience

- Spirit Baptism as the dimension of experience may occur more than once throughout your lifetime.

[Acts 19:1-7] (1) While Apollos was at Corinth, Paul took the road through the interior and arrived at Ephesus. There he found some disciples (2) and asked them, "Did you receive the Holy Spirit when you believed?" They answered, "No, we have not even heard that *there is a Holy Spirit." (3)So Paul asked, "Then what baptism did you receive?" "John's baptism," they replied. (4)Paul said, "John's baptism was a baptism of repentance. He told the people to believe in the one coming after him, that is, in Jesus." (5)On hearing this, they were baptized into the name of the Lord Jesus. (6)When Paul placed his hands on them, the Holy Spirit came on them, and they spoke in tongues and prophesied. (7)There were about twelve men in all.*

- Water Baptism will be sufficient for you to receive just once in your life, while Spirit Baptism(Fullness of the Holy Spirit) takes place in you many times.

3. You are to understand the Dual Dimension of Spirit Baptism.

- All the experiences must be contained in the contents of Union with Christ. No other experience can be exceeded more than the truth of *In Christ*.

[Eph. 1:17-19] (17)I keep asking that the God of our Lord Jesus Christ, the glorious Father, may give you the Spirit of wisdom and revelation, so that you may know him better. (18)I pray also that the eyes of your heart may be enlightened in order that you may know the hope to which he has called you, the riches of his glorious

inheritance in the saints, (19) and his incomparably great power for us who believe. That power is like the working of his mighty strength.

• How can you apply the Dual Dimensions of Spirit Baptism to your life and ministry?

ℓ. Questions for the Spiritual Ministry

1. What are two dimensions of Spirit Baptism?

_____

2. Did you experience the Spirit Baptism yet? If yes, can you share the testimony of your Spirit Baptism as the dimension of experience with others?

_____

3. Why do we need to understand the dual dimensions of Spirit Baptism?

_____

✝ Prayers of Daily Application

1. Know and meditate more about the Dual Dimension of Spirit Baptism.

2. Pray for experiencing the deeper dimension of Spirit Baptism.

Power of Spirit Baptism

1. What should you pray in order to receive the power of Spirit Baptism?

• Firstly, expect that mighty God will strengthen you with His power.

[Deut. 3:24] O Sovereign LORD, you have begun to show to your servant your greatness and your strong hand. For what god is there in heaven or on earth who can do the deeds and mighty works you do?

• Secondly, confess your sins to Jesus and be forgiven by Him.

[1 John 1:9] If we confess our sins, he is faithful and just and will *forgive us our sins and purify us from all unrighteousness.*

- Thirdly, dedicate your whole life to the Lord as a living sacrifice.

[Acts 1:4-5] (4)On one occasion, while he was eating with them, he gave them this command: "Do not leave Jerusalem, but wait for the gift my Father promised, which you have heard me speak about. (5)For John baptized with water, but in a few days you will be baptized with the Holy Spirit."

- Fourthly, believe and ask it to the Lord.

[Luke 11:13] If you then, though you are evil, know how to give good gifts to your children, how much more will your Father in heaven give the Holy Spirit to those who ask him!

2. How can you perceive that you have already received the power of Spirit Baptism?

- You will receive the Spirit Baptism by your faith, just as you also received Jesus as Lord by faith.

[Gal. 2:20] I have been crucified with Christ and I no longer live, but Christ lives in me. The life I live in the body, I live by faith in the Son of God, who loved me and gave himself for me.

- Be cautious not to be inclined to physical manifestation.
- What about then spiritual gifts such as speaking in other tongues, prophecy, dream or vision?
- Personal government of the Holy Spirit is much more important than anything else in spiritual life.

3. What are the results in your life after having received the power of Holy Spirit?

- Close intimacy with the Holy Spirit and obedience to Him

[Deut. 6:5] Love the LORD your God with all your heart and with all your soul and with all your strength.

- Growth in spirituality and becoming like Christ

[Gal. 5:22-24] (22)But the fruit of the Spirit is love, joy, peace, patience, kindness, goodness, faithfulness, (23)gentleness and self-control. Against such things there is no law. (24)Those who belong to Christ Jesus have crucified the sinful nature with its passions and desires.

- Power of evangelism and of world evangelization

[1 Cor. 2:4-5] (4)My message and my preaching were not with wise and persuasive words, but with a demonstration of the Spirit's power, (5)so that your faith might not rest on men's wisdom, but on God's power.

Questions for the Spiritual Ministry

1. What are the four steps to receive the power of Spirit Baptism?

_____

2. Explain how you are able to perceive the power of Spirit Baptism.

_____

3. What are the prominent results of being empowered by the Holy Spirit?

_____

✝ *Prayers of Daily Application*

1. Repent all the sins if you are aware of them, and make your whole being be obedient to God. And the Spirit of Christ will reign on you.

2. If you are a person who already experienced the Spirit Baptism, examine your life whether there are ongoing spiritual fruit.

NOTE

NOTE

NOTE

Lesson 7

Manifestation of the Holy Spirit and the Power

Power of the Holy Spirit and Evangelism

1. **The power of Holy Spirit must be needed in Christian life and ministry.**

[Isa. 52:7] How beautiful on the mountains are the feet of those who bring good news, who proclaim peace, who bring good tidings, who proclaim salvation, who say to Zion, "Your God reigns!"

• Holy Spirit will make you not be led by the human effort or strength but by His power.

[Rom. 8:14] because those who are led by the Spirit of God are sons of God.

2. Holy Spirit Himself is the Spirit of evangelism.

[Luke 24:48-49] (48)You are witnesses of these things. (49)I am going to send you what my Father has promised; but stay in the city until you have been clothed with power from on high.

[Acts 1:8] But you will receive power when the Holy Spirit comes on you; and you will be my witnesses in Jerusalem, and in all Judea and Samaria, and to the ends of the earth.

• Holy Spirit will lead you to the way proclaiming gospel with His manifestation and power.

[1 Cor. 2:4-5] (4)My message and my preaching were not with wise and persuasive words, but with a demonstration of the Spirit's power, (5)so that your faith might not rest on men's wisdom, but on God's power.

• Why are many Christians afraid of proclaiming Gospel? Probably one of the main reasons is that they are not familiar with the evangelism being guided by the Holy Spirit. See Philips case. He was always cautious in all his moves in accordance with the Holy Spirit. Such lifestyle was the main source of his powerful evangelism.

[Acts 8:26-40] (26)Now an angel of the Lord said to Philip, "Go south to the road--the desert road--that goes down from Jerusalem to Gaza." (27)So he started out, and on his way he met an Ethiopian eunuch, an important official in charge of all the treasury of Candace, queen of the Ethiopians. This man had gone to Jerusalem to worship, (28)and on his way home was sitting in his chariot reading the book of Isaiah the prophet. (29)The Spirit told Philip, "Go to that chariot and stay near it." (30)Then Philip ran up to the chariot and heard the man reading Isaiah the prophet. "Do you understand what you are reading?" Philip asked. (31)"How can I," he said, "unless someone explains it to me?" So he invited Philip to come up and sit with him. (32)The eunuch was reading this passage of Scripture: "He was led like a sheep to the slaughter, and as a lamb before the shearer is silent, so he did not open his mouth. (33)In his humiliation he was deprived of justice. Who can speak of his descendants? For his life was taken from the earth." (34)The eunuch asked Philip, "Tell me, please, who is the prophet talking about, himself or someone else?" (35)Then Philip began with that very passage of Scripture and told him the good news about Jesus. (36)As they traveled along the road, they came to some water and the eunuch said, "Look, here is water. Why shouldn't I be baptized?" (37)Philip said, "If you believe with all your heart, you may." The eunuch answered, "I believe that Jesus Christ is the Son of God." (38)And he gave orders to stop the chariot. Then both Philip and *the eunuch went down into the water and Philip baptized him. (39) When they came up out of the water, the Spirit of the Lord suddenly took Philip away, and the eunuch did not see him again, but went on his way rejoicing. (40) Philip, however, appeared at Azotus and traveled about, preaching the gospel in all the towns until he reached Caesarea.*

3. Ask for the enduement with the power of Holy Spirit.

• Do you really want to be empowered by the Holy Spirit? Then why? For your own pleasure or pride? For your benefit or honor? Never do that! As you know, Holy Spirit is the Spirit of God, and His gifts and power must be operated only for God as well. Therefore, we must manifest His power only for the expansion of Kingdom of Heaven.

• Before you ask Him the power from on high, you must yield yourselves as living sacrifice to God. And do not try to be controlled by the sinful nature but by the Holy Spirit at times.

[Acts 4:29-31] (29) Now, Lord, consider their threats and enable your servants to speak your word with great boldness. (30) "Stretch out your hand to heal and perform miraculous signs and wonders through the name of your holy servant Jesus." (31) After they prayed, the place where they were meeting was shaken. And they were all

filled with the Holy Spirit and spoke the word of God boldly.

• Then the Holy Spirit will use you with His power and gifts as a powerful weapon of God.

Questions for the Spiritual Ministry

1. Why do many Christians have lack of power or love in their lives and ministries?

_____

2. Why do you need the power of Holy Spirit in evangelism?

_____

3. What motive or attitude do you need as you ask the Lord to be empowered by the Holy Spirit?

_____

† *Prayers of Daily Application*

1. Ask God that the Holy Spirit will reign on you with His power of evangelism.

2. Make your mind that you should serve the Kingdom of God not with your own strength or knowledge but with the power of Holy Spirit.

Manifestation of the Holy Spirit(I)

1. Manifestation of the Holy Spirit is the work of the same Holy Spirit.

• Manifestation of the Holy Spirit; The words Holy Spirit and manifestation all take the singular form. Which means, the one and the same Holy Spirit bestows you His manifestation according to His will.

[1 Cor. 12:4-11] (4)There are different kinds of gifts, but the same Spirit. (5)There are different kinds of service, but the same Lord. (6)There are different kinds of working, but the same God works all of them in all men. (7)Now to each one the manifestation of the Spirit is given for the common good. (8)To one there is given through the Spirit the message of wisdom, to another the message *of knowledge by means of the same Spirit, (9) to another faith by the same Spirit, to another gifts of healing by that one Spirit, (10) to another miraculous powers, to another prophecy, to another distinguishing between spirits, to another speaking in different kinds of tongues, and to still another the interpretation of tongues. (11) All these are the work of one and the same Spirit, and he gives them to each one, just as he determines.*

- Never forget that the subject of the manifestation of Holy Spirit is not you but the Holy Spirit Himself.

2. Manifestation of the Holy Spirit works for the benefits of the Church.

- What does the benefit of the Church mean? Which is to say that the manifestation of Holy Spirit only works for the expansion of the Kingdom of God and for the strengthening the faith of the body of Christ, the Church.

[Rom. 1:11] I long to see you so that I may impart to you some spiritual gift to make you strong.

- No matter how much someone performs the miraculous healing, if his motive is only for his own pride and benefit, that must be selfish or demonic. Such miraculous phenomenon is quite different from that of the Holy Spirit.

> *[Jeremiah 14:14] Then the LORD said to me, "The prophets are prophesying lies in my name. I have not sent them or appointed them or spoken to them. They are prophesying to you false visions, divinations, idolatries and the delusions of their own minds.*

• An useful tip for the right discrimination whether genuine miracle or false is to examine the fruit of the tree. Fine tree always bears good fruits, and evil tree bad fruits.

3. Manifestation of the Holy Spirit works in accordance with the guidance of Holy Spirit.

> *[1 Cor. 12:11] All these are the work of one and the same Spirit, and he gives them to each one, just as he determines.*

• Key section of this sentence is *just as He determines*. Namely, the Holy Spirit will manifest His gifts and power through you according to His will by using His right method and in His right time.

• A case of an American missionary for the savage area in Africa:

The missionary, during his ministry for the area, could perform many miracles and healings among the natives.

When he met the Sabbatical year as a missionary, he ceased his ministry for a while and visited his home country. He dropped by many churches to share the missionary report with the congregation, and gave testimony about the miracles God performed through him in Africa before. After the testimony, many sick people came to the altar to receive healing prayer from him, but no miracle and healing took place there.

Such was the same in any other churches. Finally, the missionary had been too much disappointed, thinking why no miracle he could perform. Did God now forsake him? Did any sin he commit against God? He had not known the reason of it for many months.

Sometime later, after finishing his Sabbatical year in the States, he should return back to Africa even with frustrated heart. But behold! The miraculous healings and casting out demons was amazingly restarted there through his ministry!

Now, he began to realize that the manifestation of Holy Spirit is performed not by his own wish but by the will of Holy Spirit, and that the Spirit didn't want to manifest His miracles in the States, because all congregation of the churches he dropped by in the States are mostly believers. Many of them had already acknowledged God's existence.

- Likewise, you need to keep in mind that the main purpose of miracles God performs is testifying God's existence among the unbelievers.

[Acts 8:26-29] (26)Now an angel of the Lord said to Philip, "Go south to the road--the desert road--that goes down from Jerusalem to Gaza." (27)So he started out, and on his way he met an Ethiopian eunuch, an important official in charge of all the treasury of Candace, queen of the Ethiopians. This man had gone to Jerusalem to worship, (28)and on his way home was sitting in his chariot reading the book of Isaiah the prophet. (29)The Spirit told Philip, "Go to that chariot and stay near it."

[Acts 9:4-6] (4)He fell to the ground and heard a voice say to him, "Saul, Saul, why do you persecute me?" (5)"Who are you, Lord?" Saul asked. "I am Jesus, whom you are persecuting," he replied. (6) "Now get up and go into the city, and you will be told what you must do."

[Acts 9:10-16] (10)In Damascus there was a disciple named Ananias. The Lord called to him in a vision, "Ananias!" "Yes, Lord," he answered. (11)The Lord told him, "Go to the house of Judas on Straight Street and ask for a man from Tarsus named Saul, for he is praying. (12)In a vision he has seen a man named Ananias come and place his hands on him to restore his sight." (13)"Lord," Ananias answered, "I have heard many reports about this man and all the harm he has done to your saints in Jerusalem. (14)And he has come here with authority from the chief priests to arrest all who call on your name." (15)But the Lord said to Ananias, "Go! This man is my chosen instrument to carry my name before the Gentiles and their kings and before the people of Israel. (16)I will show him how much he must suffer for my name."

[Acts 10:3-6] (3)One day at about three in the afternoon he had a vision. He distinctly saw an angel of God, who came to him and said, "Cornelius!" (4)Cornelius stared at him in fear. "What is it, Lord?" he asked. The angel answered, "Your prayers and gifts to the poor have come up as a memorial offering before God. (5)Now send men to Joppa to bring back a man named Simon who is called Peter. (6)He is staying with Simon the tanner, whose house is by the sea."

[Acts 10:19-20] (19)While Peter was still thinking about the vision, the Spirit said to him, "Simon, three men are looking for you. (20) So get up and go downstairs. Do not hesitate to go with them, for I have sent them."

[Acts 12:7-9] (7)Suddenly an angel of the Lord appeared and a light shone in the cell. He struck Peter on the side and woke him up. "Quick, get up!" he said, and the chains fell off Peter's wrists. (8)Then the angel said to him, "Put on your clothes and sandals." And Peter did so. "Wrap your cloak around you and follow me," the angel told him. (9)Peter followed him out of the prison, but he had no idea that what the angel was doing was really happening; he thought he was seeing a vision.

[Acts 20:23] I only know that in every city the Holy Spirit warns me that prison and hardships are facing me.

[Acts 21:4] Finding the disciples there, we stayed with them seven days. Through the Spirit they urged Paul not to go on to Jerusalem.

Questions for the Spiritual Ministry

1. Why does the Holy Spirit distribute his gifts or manifestation not same to all believers?

_____

2. Some believers seem to have spiritual manifestation, and others not. Then why does the Holy Spirit make a difference between

them?

_____

3. Have you ever heard the case like the story of the American missionary above? If yes, share with us.

_____

✝ Prayers of Daily Application

1. Pray for the manifestation of Holy Spirit only for the benefit of the Church.

2. Try to keep walking with the Holy Spirit so that you can perform the manifestation of Holy Spirit by His guidance.

Manifestation of the Holy Spirit(II)

1. Manifestation of the Holy Spirit through realization

• There are 3 divisions in the way of manifesting the power of Holy Spirit; First one of these is the manifestation through realization. There also 3 gifts of the manifestation of Holy Spirit through realization are introduced in 1 Cor. 12:8-11; One of these is the gift of the word of wisdom.

> [1 Cor. 12:8-11] (8) To one there is given through the Spirit the message of wisdom, to another the message of knowledge by means of the same Spirit, (9) to another faith by the same Spirit, to another gifts of healing by that one Spirit, (10) to another miraculous powers, to another prophecy, to another distinguishing between spirits, to another speaking in different kinds of tongues, and to still

another the interpretation of tongues. (11)*All these are the work of one and the same Spirit, and he gives them to each one, just as he determines.*

- The gift of the word of wisdom is very important manifestation for all the preachers and lay leaders as they are meditating Bible, preaching and teaching the word of God.

[Acts 2:14-36] (14)Then Peter stood up with the Eleven, raised his voice and addressed the crowd: "Fellow Jews and all of you who live in Jerusalem, let me explain this to you; listen carefully to what I say. (15)These men are not drunk, as you suppose. It's only nine in the morning!" (16)No, this is what was spoken by the prophet Joel: (17)"'In the last days, God says, I will pour out my Spirit on all people. Your sons and daughters will prophesy, your young men will see visions, your old men will dream dreams. (18)Even on my servants, both men and women, I will pour out my Spirit in those days, and they will prophesy. (19)I will show wonders in the heaven above and signs on the earth below, blood and fire and billows of smoke. (20)The sun will be turned to darkness and the moon to blood before the coming of the great and glorious day of the Lord. (21)And everyone who calls on the name of the Lord will be saved.'" (22)"Men of Israel, listen to this: Jesus of Nazareth was a man accredited by God to you by miracles, wonders and signs,

which God did among you through him, as you yourselves know. (23) This man was handed over to you by God's set purpose and foreknowledge; and you, with the help of wicked men, put him to death by nailing him to the cross. (24) But God raised him from the dead, freeing him from the agony of death, because it was impossible for death to keep its hold on him. (25) David said about him: "'I saw the Lord always before me. Because he is at my right hand, I will not be shaken. (26) Therefore my heart is glad and my tongue rejoices; my body also will live in hope, (27) because you will not abandon me to the grave, nor will you let your Holy One see decay. (28) You have made known to me the paths of life; you will fill me with joy in your presence.'" (29) "Brothers, I can tell you confidently that the patriarch David died and was buried, and his tomb is here to this day. (30) But he was a prophet and knew that God had promised him on oath that he would place one of his descendants on his throne. (31) Seeing what was ahead, he spoke of the resurrection of the Christ, that he was not abandoned to the grave, nor did his body see decay. (32) God has raised this Jesus to life, and we are all witnesses of the fact. (33) Exalted to the right hand of God, he has received from the Father the promised Holy Spirit and has poured out what you now see and hear. (34) For David did not ascend to heaven, and yet he said, "'The Lord said to my Lord: "Sit at my right hand (35) until I make your enemies a footstool for your feet.'" (36) "Therefore let all Israel be assured of this: God has made this Jesus, whom you crucified, both Lord and Christ."

[Acts 6:10] but they could not stand up against his wisdom or the Spirit by whom he spoke.

[Acts 26:13-18] (13) About noon, O king, as I was on the road, I saw a light from heaven, brighter than the sun, blazing around me and my companions. (14) We all fell to the ground, and I heard a voice saying to me in Aramaic, 'Saul, Saul, why do you persecute me? It is hard for you to kick against the goads.' (15) "Then I asked, 'Who are you, Lord?' "'I am Jesus, whom you are persecuting,' the Lord replied. (16) 'Now get up and stand on your feet. I have appeared to you to appoint you as a servant and as a witness of what you have seen of me and what I will show you. (17) I will rescue you from your own people and from the Gentiles. I am sending you to them (18) to open their eyes and turn them from darkness to light, and from the power of Satan to God, so that they may receive forgiveness of sins and a place among those who are sanctified by faith in me.'

- The second of the manifestation of Holy Spirit through realization is the gift of the word of knowledge. Which is the manifestation that you will sometimes perceive the inner secret of hidden things or environment beyond your understanding. The case of Ananias and Sapphira;

[Acts 5:1-11] (1) Now a man named Ananias, together with his wife Sapphira, also sold a piece of property. (2) With his wife's full knowledge he kept back part of the money for himself, but brought the rest and put it at the apostles' feet. (3) Then Peter said, "Ananias, how is it that Satan has so filled your heart that you have lied to the Holy Spirit and have kept for yourself some of the money you received for the land? (4) Didn't it belong to you before it was sold? And after it was sold, wasn't the money at your disposal? What made you think of doing such a thing? You have not lied to men but to God." (5) When Ananias heard this, he fell down and died. And great fear seized all who heard what had happened. (6) Then the young men came forward, wrapped up his body, and carried him out and buried him. (7) About three hours later his wife came in, not knowing what had happened. (8) Peter asked her, "Tell me, is this the price you and Ananias got for the land?" "Yes," she said, "that is the price." (9) Peter said to her, "How could you agree to test the Spirit of the Lord? Look! The feet of the men who buried your husband are at the door, and they will carry you out also." (10) At that moment she fell down at his feet and died. Then the young men came in and, finding her dead, carried her out and buried her beside her husband. (11) Great fear seized the whole church and all

who heard about these events.

- The third is discriminating spirits. Discriminating spirits of other persons or things by the supernatural perception given by the Holy Spirit. Mostly the Holy Spirit gives it to you by using the method of vision, symbol or prophecy in time of your intercession for others.

[Acts 8:23] For I see that you are full of bitterness and captive to sin.

[1 Cor. 14:29] Two or three prophets should speak, and the others should weigh carefully what is said.

2. Manifestation of the Holy Spirit through utterance

- The second division is the manifestation of Holy Spirit through utterance. There are 3 in this; Prophecy, speaking in other tongues and the interpretation of tongues.
- The gift of prophecy is for edifying believers and for strengthening the church.

[1 Cor. 14:1] Follow the way of love and eagerly desire spiritual gifts, especially the gift of prophecy.

[1 Cor. 14:3] But everyone who prophesies speaks to men for their strengthening, encouragement and comfort.

[1 Cor. 14:4] He who speaks in a tongue edifies himself, but he who prophesies edifies the church.

[1 Cor. 14:22] Tongues, then, are a sign, not for believers but for unbelievers; prophecy, however, is for believers, not for unbelievers.

- You will need to pant for the gift of prophecy.

[1 Cor. 14:39] Therefore, my brothers, be eager to prophesy, and do not forbid speaking in tongues.

- The gift of prophecy will be frequently occurred in your praying, preaching and counselling for other.

[Acts 13:9-11] (9) Then Saul, who was also called Paul, filled with the Holy Spirit, looked straight at Elymas and said, (10) "You are a child of the devil and an enemy of everything that is right! You are full of all kinds of deceit and trickery. Will you never stop perverting the right ways of the Lord? (11) Now the hand of the Lord is against you. You are going to be blind, and for a time you will be unable to

see the light of the sun." Immediately mist and darkness came over him, and he groped about, seeking someone to lead him by the hand.

[Acts 19:6] When Paul placed his hands on them, the Holy Spirit came on them, and they spoke in tongues and prophesied.

[Acts 21:9-11] (9)He had four unmarried daughters who prophesied. (10)After we had been there a number of days, a prophet named Agabus came down from Judea. (11)Coming over to us, he took Paul's belt, tied his own hands and feet with it and said, "The Holy Spirit says, 'In this way the Jews of Jerusalem will bind the owner of this belt and will hand him over to the Gentiles.'"

[Acts 27:10] "Men, I can see that our voyage is going to be disastrous and bring great loss to ship and cargo, and to our own lives also."

[Acts 27:22-26] (22)But now I urge you to keep up your courage, because not one of you will be lost; only the ship will be destroyed. (23)Last night an angel of the God whose I am and whom I serve stood beside me (24)and said, 'Do not be afraid, Paul. You must stand trial before Caesar; and God has graciously given you the lives of all who sail with you.' (25)So keep up your courage, men, for I have faith in God that it will happen just as he told me. (26)

Nevertheless, we must run aground on some island.

• Speaking in other tongues is the second gift of the manifestation of Holy Spirit through utterance.

[Acts 2:4] All of them were filled with the Holy Spirit and began to speak in other tongues as the Spirit enabled them.

[Acts 10:46] For they heard them speaking in tongues and praising God. Then Peter said,

[Acts 19:6] When Paul placed his hands on them, the Holy Spirit came on them, and they spoke in tongues and prophesied.

[1 Cor. 14:2] For anyone who speaks in a tongue does not speak to men but to God. Indeed, no one understands him; he utters mysteries with his spirit.

[1 Cor. 14:23] So if the whole church comes together and everyone speaks in tongues, and some who do not understand or some unbelievers come in, will they not say that you are out of your mind?

[1 Cor. 14:39] Therefore, my brothers, be eager to prophesy, and

do not forbid speaking in tongues.

• But your consciousness cannot perceive what the subconsciousness expresses through speaking in other tongues. That's why the Bible exhorts that you should pray for the interpretation of it.

[1 Cor. 14:13] For this reason anyone who speaks in a tongue should pray that he may interpret what he says.

• When the Holy Spirit manifest the interpretation of tongues, you are able to understand within your consciousness what you are speaking in other tongues.

[1 Cor. 14:5] I would like every one of you to speak in tongues, but I would rather have you prophesy. He who prophesies is greater than one who speaks in tongues, unless he interprets, so that the church may be edified.

[1 Cor. 14:13-15] (13) For this reason anyone who speaks in a tongue should pray that he may interpret what he says. (14) For if I pray in a tongue, my spirit prays, but my mind is unfruitful. (15) So what shall I do? I will pray with my spirit, but I will also pray with my mind; I will sing with my spirit, but I will also sing with my mind.

[1 Cor. 14:26-28] (26) What then shall we say, brothers? When you come together, everyone has a hymn, or a word of instruction,

a revelation, a tongue or an interpretation. All of these must be done for the strengthening of the church. (27)If anyone speaks in a tongue, two--or at the most three--should speak, one at a time, and someone must interpret. (28)If there is no interpreter, the speaker should keep quiet in the church and speak to himself and God.

- When you are aware of interpretation in your mind during your speaking in tongues, and if your congregation wants to hear from you, tell the interpretation in accordance with the spiritual guidance. It will give others strength and comfort that come from God.

3. Manifestation of the Holy Spirit through the act of faith

- The third division of the manifestation of Holy Spirit is that of through the act of faith. Which contains the gift of faith, of healing and of power.
- The gift of faith is not the ordinary faith but the special faith that can even perform the miracles. Such faith is given by the Holy Spirit for the special purpose.

[Acts 3:1-16] (1)One day Peter and John were going up to the

temple at the time of prayer--at three in the afternoon. (2) Now a man crippled from birth was being carried to the temple gate called Beautiful, where he was put every day to beg from those going into the temple courts. (3) When he saw Peter and John about to enter, he asked them for money. (4) Peter looked straight at him, as did John. Then Peter said, "Look at us!" (5) So the man gave them his attention, expecting to get something from them. (6) Then Peter said, "Silver or gold I do not have, but what I have I give you. In the name of Jesus Christ of Nazareth, walk." (7) Taking him by the right hand, he helped him up, and instantly the man's feet and ankles became strong. (8) He jumped to his feet and began to walk. Then he went with them into the temple courts, walking and jumping, and praising God. (9) When all the people saw him walking and praising God, (10) they recognized him as the same man who used to sit begging at the temple gate called Beautiful, and they were filled with wonder and amazement at what had happened to him. (11) While the beggar held on to Peter and John, all the people were astonished and came running to them in the place called Solomon's Colonnade. (12) When Peter saw this, he said to them: "Men of Israel, why does this surprise you? Why do you stare at us as if by our own power or godliness we had made this man walk? (13) The God of Abraham, Isaac and Jacob, the God of our fathers, has glorified his servant Jesus. You handed him over to be killed, and you disowned him before Pilate, though he had decided to let him go. (14)You disowned the Holy and Righteous One and asked that a murderer be released to you. (15)You killed the author of life, but God raised him from the dead. We are witnesses of this. (16)By faith in the name of Jesus, this man whom you see and know was made strong. It is Jesus' name and the faith that comes through him that has given this complete healing to him, as you can all see.

[Acts 9:33-35] (33)There he found a man named Aeneas, a paralytic who had been bedridden for eight years. (34)"Aeneas," Peter said to him, "Jesus Christ heals you. Get up and take care of your mat." Immediately Aeneas got up. (35)All those who lived in Lydda and Sharon saw him and turned to the Lord.

[Acts 14:8-10] (8)In Lystra there sat a man crippled in his feet, who was lame from birth and had never walked. (9)He listened to Paul as he was speaking. Paul looked directly at him, saw that he had faith to be healed (10)and called out, "Stand up on your feet!" At that, the man jumped up and began to walk.

- The gift of healing is only for curing disease. The gift of healing is similar, in some sense, with that of faith and of power.

[Acts 4:30] Stretch out your hand to heal and perform miraculous signs and wonders through the name of your holy servant Jesus.

[Acts 5:16] Crowds gathered also from the towns around Jerusalem, bringing their sick and those tormented by evil spirits, and all of them were healed.

[Acts 28:8-9] (8)His father was sick in bed, suffering from fever and dysentery. Paul went in to see him and, after prayer, placed his hands on him and healed him. (9)When this had happened, the rest of the sick on the island came and were cured.

• When one can perform miracle by the guidance of Holy Spirit during proclaiming gospel, that must be the manifestation of the gift of power.

[Acts 2:43] Everyone was filled with awe, and many wonders and miraculous signs were done by the apostles.

[Acts 5:12] The apostles performed many miraculous signs and wonders among the people. And all the believers used to meet together in Solomon's Colonnade.

[Acts 6:8] Now Stephen, a man full of God's grace and power, did great wonders and miraculous signs among the people.

[Acts 8:12-13] (12)But when they believed Philip as he preached *the good news of the kingdom of God and the name of Jesus Christ, they were baptized, both men and women. (13) Simon himself believed and was baptized. And he followed Philip everywhere, astonished by the great signs and miracles he saw.*

[Acts 9:36-40] (36) In Joppa there was a disciple named Tabitha (which, when translated, is Dorcas), who was always doing good and helping the poor. (37) About that time she became sick and died, and her body was washed and placed in an upstairs room. (38) Lydda was near Joppa; so when the disciples heard that Peter was in Lydda, they sent two men to him and urged him, "Please come at once!" (39) Peter went with them, and when he arrived he was taken upstairs to the room. All the widows stood around him, crying and showing him the robes and other clothing that Dorcas had made while she was still with them. (40) Peter sent them all out of the room; then he got down on his knees and prayed. Turning toward the dead woman, he said, "Tabitha, get up." She opened her eyes, and seeing Peter she sat up.

[Acts 14:3] So Paul and Barnabas spent considerable time there, speaking boldly for the Lord, who confirmed the message of his grace by enabling them to do miraculous signs and wonders.

[Acts 16:16-18] (16) Once when we were going to the place of

prayer, we were met by a slave girl who had a spirit by which she predicted the future. She earned a great deal of money for her owners by fortune-telling. (17) This girl followed Paul and the rest of us, shouting, "These men are servants of the Most High God, who are telling you the way to be saved." (18) She kept this up for many days. Finally Paul became so troubled that he turned around and said to the spirit, "In the name of Jesus Christ I command you to come out of her!" At that moment the spirit left her.

[Acts 19:11-12] (11) God did extraordinary miracles through Paul, (12) so that even handkerchiefs and aprons that had touched him were taken to the sick, and their illnesses were cured and the evil spirits left them.

[Acts 20:10] Paul went down, threw himself on the young man and put his arms around him. "Don't be alarmed," he said. "He's alive!"

[Acts 28:3-6] (3) Paul gathered a pile of brushwood and, as he put it on the fire, a viper, driven out by the heat, fastened itself on his hand. (4) When the islanders saw the snake hanging from his hand, they said to each other, "This man must be a murderer; for though he escaped from the sea, Justice has not allowed him to live." (5) But Paul shook the snake off into the fire and suffered no ill effects. (6) The people expected him to swell up or suddenly fall dead, but

after waiting a long time and seeing nothing unusual happen to him, they changed their minds and said he was a god.

• Don't forget that all the gifts and manifestation of Holy Spirit of which owner is the Holy Spirit, and that the gifts are manifested only by the guidance of Holy Spirit. First thing you need to prepare before you are used by the Holy Spirit is, therefore, to discern the accurate guidance of Holy Spirit in all you do. Always keep in mind that the purpose of the manifestation of Holy Spirit is only for the benefit of the Church, namely, only for proclaiming Gospel and for edifying the body of Christ.

❦ Questions for the Spiritual Ministry

1. Enumerate the examples of Spiritual gifts or manifestation recorded in 1 Cor. 12:8-11.

_____

2. What are the three dimensions of the manifestation of Holy Spirit?

_____

3. What attitude must you need before you perform the manifestation of Holy Spirit?

_____

✝ Prayers of Daily Application

1. Are you aware what spiritual gifts the Holy Spirit manifest through your ministry?

2. Pray that the more abundant manifestation of Holy Spirit will be performed in your life and service.

Holy Spirit and Glossolalia

1. Some reject Glossolalia itself.

- Glossolalia, in other words, speaking in other tongues, has been the one of the hottest issues of Pneumatology nowaday.
- There are some theologians who have very strong negative viewpoint on this matter. Many of Reformed-line theologians deny the existence of glossolalia today, for they believe all the special gifts such as glossolalia, prophecy, divine healing were already ceased at the close of the Apostolic age.

> [1 Cor. 13:8] Love never fails. But where there are prophecies, they will cease; where there are tongues, they will be stilled; where there is knowledge, it will pass away.

• Traditional Wesleyan-Holiness line also rejects glossolalia, for they much more stress purity and power rather than that. However, there were some sectarians who fierily advocated glossolalia in Wesleyan-Holiness line in the late nineteenth century, and they finally seceded from their main Wesleyan-Holiness wing.

2. Some regard Glossolalia as the accurate sign of Spirit Baptism.

[Acts 2:1-4] (1) When the day of Pentecost came, they were all together in one place. (2) Suddenly a sound like the blowing of a violent wind came from heaven and filled the whole house where they were sitting. (3) They saw what seemed to be tongues of fire that separated and came to rest on each of them. (4) All of them were filled with the Holy Spirit and began to speak in other tongues as the Spirit enabled them.

• To this day, the denominational statement of Pentecostal churches affirms that glossolalia is the accurate sign of Spirit Baptism.

[Acts 10:44-46] (44) While Peter was still speaking these words, the Holy Spirit came on all who heard the message. (45) The

circumcised believers who had come with Peter were astonished that the gift of the Holy Spirit had been poured out even on the Gentiles. (46)For they heard them speaking in tongues and praising God. Then Peter said,

3. Some regard Glossolalia as one of the Spiritual gifts.

• As for the Third Wavers, most of them believe glossolalia is one of the spiritual gifts rather than the accurate sign of Spirit Baptism. Such tendency has probably taken place in charismatic reformed-line believers who accept spiritual gifts but not allowing it as the sign of Spirit Baptism.

[1 Cor. 12:8-11] (8)To one there is given through the Spirit the message of wisdom, to another the message of knowledge by means of the same Spirit, (9)to another faith by the same Spirit, to another gifts of healing by that one Spirit, (10)to another miraculous powers, to another prophecy, to another distinguishing between spirits, to another speaking in different kinds of tongues, and to still another the interpretation of tongues. (11)All these are the work of one and the same Spirit, and he gives them to each one, just as he determines.

• Interestingly, many of young Pentecostal pastors also like to express such conviction above rather than their traditional doctrinal confession. Likewise, Reformed and Wesleyan-Holiness line nowaday seem to access to that way more than they did before.

❡ Questions for the Spiritual Ministry

1. Why do some theologians nowaday reject glossolalia as spiritual gifts?

___

2. What doctrinal statement of denomination affirm that the speaking in other tongues is the accurate sign of Spirit Baptism?

___

3. Explain the recent tendency in modern churches how they deal with the manifestation of glossolalia.

___

† *Prayers of Daily Application*

1. Have you ever had any negative position on the speaking in other tongues? Pray for your clearer understanding of the biblical statement on it.

2. If you are able to speak in other tongues, pray and try that you will get more benefits and strength for your spiritual improvement through practicing it.

NOTE

NOTE

NOTE

Lesson 8

Holy Spirit and the Healing

01

Holy Spirit and the Holistic Healing

1. Holy Spirit heals human spirit.

• Human being, originally, have been ruined by sin since Adam's fall. The severe disease of depravity has infected whole sphere of human existence including body, soul and spirit. However, God sent His only Son Jesus Christ, and let him sacrificed himself for the remedy of all human sins and diseases. So Jesus Christ really wants to heal your all wounded spirit and soul and body as a whole. This we call holistic healing.

[1 Thess. 5:23-24] (23)May God himself, the God of peace, sanctify you through and through. May your whole spirit, soul and body be kept blameless at the coming of our Lord Jesus Christ. (24) The one who calls you is faithful and he will do it.

• As for the healing of your spirit, the healing takes place when your spirit is awakened by new birth through the influence of the Holy Spirit.

[Rom. 1:21] For although they knew God, they neither glorified him as God nor gave thanks to him, but their thinking became futile and their foolish hearts were darkened.

2. Holy Spirit heals human soul.

• Jesus Christ wants to heal not just only your spirit but also your soul. You can serve the Lord wholeheartedly only when your soul is dedicated to him as a living sacrifice. The main functions of your soul are intelligence, emotion and free will. These functions must be obedient to the Lord first, if you really want to experience the healing for soul.

• As for the healing for soul, it is gradual and life-long process, while the healing for spirit, regeneration, instantaneously occurs. Healing for soul first needs the repentance of sin. Without repentance, no one can be cured or purified by God.

• The second required condition for healing is your full dedication to God. God's holy healing will begin to reign on you, but only after you have absolutely devoted yourself to the Lord. You can experience the instantaneous sanctification of heart as you offer yourself to God with cordial repentance and full surrender.

> [Rom. 6:6] For we know that our old self was crucified with him so that the body of sin might be done away with, that we should no longer be slaves to sin.

> [Gal. 5:24] Those who belong to Christ Jesus have crucified the sinful nature with its passions and desires.

• The healing for soul, sanctification, is only based on the truth that Jesus was crucified for your salvation.

3. Holy Spirit heals human body.

• Since human body is very connected with soul, it is so natural that the symptoms of soul are mostly revealed in the body. You will know that if you examine your bodily condition whether good or bad when the time you are very glad or sad in soul.

> [Exodus 15:26] He said, "If you listen carefully to the voice of the LORD your God and do what is right in his eyes, if you pay attention to his commands and keep all his decrees, I will not bring on you any of the diseases I brought on the Egyptians, for I am the LORD, who heals you."

- Physical disease or sickness frequently takes place when your soul is not in order. In this case, taking medicine or surgery is not enough for the complete recovery. Since the origin of the disease comes from the soul, for the full treatment, your soul must be cured first of all by God. Because, God wants you to be healed holistically.

> *[1 Thess. 5:23] May God himself, the God of peace, sanctify you through and through. May your whole spirit, soul and body be kept blameless at the coming of our Lord Jesus Christ.*

Questions for the Spiritual Ministry

1. Describe the meaning of Holistic Healing.

_____

2. Compare the healing for soul with healing for spirit.

_____

3. Present some examples that the function of human body is very closely connected with his soul, especially in the case of disease.

✝ Prayers of Daily Application

1. Are you now sick in bed, or sometimes are you not in good health? Why don't you ask the Lord whether He has an specific instruction for you?

2. Pray for the holistic health of your body and soul and spirit, and for your faithful devotion unto the Lord with the health.

Inner Healing

1. Holy Spirit wants believer's inner healing.

• God's will for the believers in trials

• Inner healing is, positively saying, the process of holiness throughout the life-long journey.

[2 Cor. 1:8-9] (8)We do not want you to be uninformed, brothers, about the hardships we suffered in the province of Asia. We were under great pressure, far beyond our ability to endure, so that we despaired even of life. (9)Indeed, in our hearts we felt the sentence of death. But this happened that we might not rely on ourselves but on God, who raises the dead.

[James 1:2-4] (2)Consider it pure joy, my brothers, whenever you *face trials of many kinds, (3) because you know that the testing of your faith develops perseverance. (4) Perseverance must finish its work so that you may be mature and complete, not lacking anything.*

2. How does the inner healing take place in human soul?

• Why do you need the healing of the sorrowful emotions and bad memories in your heart?

[Gal. 5:19-21] (19) The acts of the sinful nature are obvious: sexual immorality, impurity and debauchery; (20) idolatry and witchcraft; hatred, discord, jealousy, fits of rage, selfish ambition, dissensions, factions (21) and envy; drunkenness, orgies, and the like. I warn you, as I did before, that those who live like this will not inherit the kingdom of God.

• Inner healing takes place, more than over, as you forgive your or others broken emotions and bitter memories.

3. You can experience the inner healing by the power and guidance of Holy Spirit.

• Through prayer, the Holy Spirit uncovers the hidden things in your heart and enables you to make the sound relationship with the Lord.

• Healing takes place as you yield your sins and pains unto Jesus' cross.

• The more you are healed, the more you can be governed by God's reign.

[Col. 2:15] And having disarmed the powers and authorities, he made a public spectacle of them, triumphing over them by the cross.

[James 4:7] Submit yourselves, then, to God. Resist the devil, and he will flee from you.

[1 Peter 5:9] Resist him, standing firm in the faith, because you know that your brothers throughout the world are undergoing the same kind of sufferings..

Questions for the Spiritual Ministry

1. Why do you need the inner healing?

2. Share your testimonies of inner healing, if you have any.

_____

3. How can you help others through the guidance of Holy Spirit for their inner healing?

_____

† *Prayers of Daily Application*

1. Let the Holy Spirit search your heart so that He could reveal the hidden darkness that must be eradicated in you.

2. Pray concretely for the persons around you who will need their inner healing.

Holy Spirit and Dream

1. General understanding on dream

• There are various kinds of dream; Dream takes place in your unconsciousness, and the general dream mostly takes place according to the physical and psychological experiences in daily life.

• Analysing dream, that will need your specialized understanding and training. Otherwise, that might bring an evil influence to you or to others.

[Joel 2:28-29] (28)And afterward, I will pour out my Spirit on all people. Your sons and daughters will prophesy, your old men will dream dreams, your young men will see visions. (29)Even on my servants, both men and women, I will pour out my Spirit in those *days.*

• When you need to analyze the dream, you have to deal it with the viewpoint of healing and restoration of your body and soul.

2. Biblical understanding on dream
• There are many instances of the altruistic dreams in the Bible.
• When someone dreams an altruistic dream, that dream can be utilized for the evangelism and for the benefit of the church through the life and ministry of devoted Christians.

[Gen. 28:10-17] (10)Jacob left Beersheba and set out for Haran. (11)When he reached a certain place, he stopped for the night because the sun had set. Taking one of the stones there, he put it under his head and lay down to sleep. (12)He had a dream in which he saw a stairway resting on the earth, with its top reaching to heaven, and the angels of God were ascending and descending on it. (13)There above it stood the LORD, and he said: "I am the LORD, the God of your father Abraham and the God of Isaac. I will give you and your descendants the land on which you are lying. (14)Your descendants will be like the dust of the earth, and you will spread out to the west and to the east, to the north and to the south. All peoples on earth will be blessed through you and your

offspring. (15)I am with you and will watch over you wherever you go, and I will bring you back to this land. I will not leave you until I have done what I have promised you." (16)When Jacob awoke from his sleep, he thought, "Surely the LORD is in this place, and I was not aware of it." (17)He was afraid and said, "How awesome is this place! This is none other than the house of God; this is the gate of heaven."

[Matt. 2:13-22] (13)When they had gone, an angel of the Lord appeared to Joseph in a dream.." Get up," he said, "take the child and his mother and escape to Egypt. Stay there until I tell you, for Herod is going to search for the child to kill him." (14)So he got up, took the child and his mother during the night and left for Egypt, (15)where he stayed until the death of Herod. And so was fulfilled what the Lord had said through the prophet: "Out of Egypt I called my son." (16)When Herod realized that he had been outwitted by the Magi, he was furious, and he gave orders to kill all the boys in Bethlehem and its vicinity who were two years old and under, in accordance with the time he had learned from the Magi. (17)Then what was said through the prophet Jeremiah was fulfilled: (18)"A voice is heard in Ramah, weeping and great mourning, Rachel weeping for her children and refusing to be comforted, because they are no more." (19)After Herod died, an angel of the Lord appeared in a dream to Joseph in Egypt (20)and said, "Get up, take *the child and his mother and go to the land of Israel, for those who were trying to take the child's life are dead." (21) So he got up, took the child and his mother and went to the land of Israel. (22) But when he heard that Archelaus was reigning in Judea in place of his father Herod, he was afraid to go there. Having been warned in a dream, he withdrew to the district of Galilee.*

[Luke 1:36-40] (36) "Even Elizabeth your relative is going to have a child in her old age, and she who was said to be barren is in her sixth month. (37) For nothing is impossible with God." (38) "I am the Lord's servant," Mary answered. "May it be to me as you have said." Then the angel left her. (39) At that time Mary got ready and hurried to a town in the hill country of Judea, (40) where she entered Zechariah's home and greeted Elizabeth.

[Acts 2:17] In the last days, God says, I will pour out my Spirit on all people. Your sons and daughters will prophesy, your young men will see visions, your old men will dream dreams.

3. Theological understanding on dream

- The function of healing and restoration in regard of dreaming
- The right attitude of analyzing dreams should be for your spiritual improvement. See Jacob's case:

[Gen. 28:12, 16-17] (12) He had a dream in which he saw a stairway resting on the earth, with its top reaching to heaven, and the angels of God were ascending and descending on it. (16) When Jacob awoke from his sleep, he thought, "Surely the LORD is in this place, and I was not aware of it." (17) He was afraid and said, "How awesome is this place! This is none other than the house of God; this is the gate of heaven."

Questions for the Spiritual Ministry

1. What will be the reason why you dream almost every night?

_____

2. Do you have any altruistic dream that you have remembered?

_____

3. Choose one of the dreams you dreamed, and apply its theological analysis to your spiritual improvement.

_____

✝ Prayers of Daily Application

1. Are there any persons around you who are frequently afflicted with evil dreams? Pray for their inner healing and restoration.

2. There may be people who fail to have right explanation on their dreaming. Guide them to the evangelical understanding on it.

04

Physical Healing

1. What attitude should Christians need when they catch disease?

• Giving thanks to the Lord, which is the attitude you should have at the first time when you are aware that you catched a disease.

• You can get either instruction for your spiritual repentance or realization that you need some rest for your body. Sometimes you may have to improve your environment.

> [Exodus 15:26] He said, "If you listen carefully to the voice of the LORD your God and do what is right in his eyes, if you pay attention to his commands and keep all his decrees, I will not bring on you any of the diseases I brought on the Egyptians, for I am the LORD, who heals you."

[Phil. 4:6-7] (6) Do not be anxious about anything, but in everything, by prayer and petition, with thanksgiving, present your requests to God. (7) And the peace of God, which transcends all understanding, will guard your hearts and your minds in Christ Jesus.

[James 5:15-16] (15) And the prayer offered in faith will make the sick person well; the Lord will raise him up. If he has sinned, he will be forgiven. (16) Therefore confess your sins to each other and pray for each other so that you may be healed. The prayer of a righteous man is powerful and effective.

2. False teachings on physical healing

• Some teachers say that all the sickness and pains come from Devil, and that it is God's will for all to be healed without exception.
• Some have a misbelief that it is not the way of Christian belief to use medicine or medical treatment.
• Some teachers have a haughty spirit, believing themselves as a miracle-doer who can perform miraculous healing whenever they want to heal diseases of others.

[Acts 3:12] When Peter saw this, he said to them: "Men of Israel, why does this surprise you? Why do you stare at us as if by our own power or godliness we had made this man walk?"

3. Evangelical attitude on physical healing

• The fundamental faith that all the Christians need is the conviction that the body and soul of Christians are no more for themselves. They are already holy temple and mighty weapon of God. Declare it!

• You don't need to recognize the symptom of sickness and pain unless you are able to convinced the will of God for the disease. Resist the Devil!

> [Mal. 4:2] But for you who revere my name, the sun of righteousness will rise with healing in its wings. And you will go out and leap like calves released from the stall.

> [John 10:10] The thief comes only to steal and kill and destroy; I have come that they may have life, and have it to the full.

> [James 4:7] Submit yourselves, then, to God. Resist the devil, and he will flee from you.

> [1 Peter 2:24] He himself bore our sins in his body on the tree, so that we might die to sins and live for righteousness; by his wounds you have been healed.

ℓ. Questions for the Spiritual Ministry

1. What must you do when you are sick in bed before you ask to the Lord to be healed?

_____

2. Enumerate some misbeliefs on divine healing.

_____

3. Do you know some valuable scripture verses for divine healing?

_____

† Prayers of Daily Application

1. What do you do when you are sick in bed? Confess that your body is not yours but God's. And pray to be guided by the Holy Spirit. He will give you conviction while you are praying.

2. Pray for the sicks, especially pray for them with the guidance of Holy Spirit.

Holy Spirit and Evil Spirits

1. What are demons?

- Devil(διαβολος): singular number
- demons(δαιμονια): plural number

[Matt. 9:32-34] (32)While they were going out, a man who was demon-possessed and could not talk was brought to Jesus. (33)And when the demon was driven out, the man who had been mute spoke. The crowd was amazed and said, "Nothing like this has ever been seen in Israel." (34)But the Pharisees said, "It is by the prince of demons that he drives out demons."

2. What is demon-possessed?

• When people are possessed by demons, their unconsciousness and awareness may be handled by demons. However, as for the case of born-again Christians, the Holy Spirit keeps their spirit secure from demon's infiltration.

• Unlike demon-possessed, the born-again Christians may be influenced by demons anytime, which is demon-influenced, if they are not filled with the Holy Spirit.

> [Luke 11:24-26] (24) "When an evil spirit comes out of a man, it goes through arid places seeking rest and does not find it. Then it says, 'I will return to the house I left.' (25) When it arrives, it finds the house swept clean and put in order. (26) Then it goes and takes seven other spirits more wicked than itself, and they go in and live there. And the final condition of that man is worse than the first."

3. You are able to defeat the demonic forces by the power of Holy Spirit.

• Misbelief that all the diseases come from demons, and that the exorcism can only cure the psychological and physical sickness; Such conviction is too narrow-minded.

• Misbelief that the medical examination and treatment is not the biblical tools, and that only with prayer God can heal; But God also likes to use the medical treatment as well as prayer.

• Misbelief that the special gift of healing can be afforded only to the particular person; But the Bible tells us that all the Christians have power to demolish the demonic influence.

[Mark 16:17] And these signs will accompany those who believe: In my name they will drive out demons; they will speak in new tongues.

Questions for the Spiritual Ministry

1. Contrast demons with Devil.

___

2. Is there any difference between demon-possessed and demon-influenced?

___

3. Introduce some misbeliefs on the practice of exorcism.

___

✝ Prayers of Daily Application

1. You will need the sound biblical discernment to discriminate between demon-possession and mental illness. Pray for that.

2. Prepare yourself that you can be used as God's tool especially for delivering the demon-possessed or demon-influenced from their terrible oppression.

NOTE

NOTE

NOTE

Lesson 9
Pneumatology and the Radical Spiritual Movement

Various Types of the Radical Spiritual Movements

1. **Modern churches face with much difficulties in terms of discriminating the radical spiritualism.**

• Since each denomination has its own doctrinal standpoint, it is very difficult for us to come to a conclusion whether a certain suspicious group is orthodox or heresy.

[2 Tim. 2:15] Do your best to present yourself to God as one approved, a workman who does not need to be ashamed and who correctly handles the word of truth.

• Some groups that were once rejected as heresy could be recognized as orthodox nowaday. While they are still rejected as heresy by many other denominations, on the contrary, they might be welcomed by some other different denominations.

> [2 Thess. 2:9-10] (9) The coming of the lawless one will be in accordance with the work of Satan displayed in all kinds of counterfeit miracles, signs and wonders, (10) and in every sort of evil that deceives those who are perishing. They perish because they refused to love the truth and so be saved.

2. We need the unified institution for examining heresies in order to discriminate the radical spiritualism.

- However, abstain from partial and narrow-minded estimation which is too much inclined to the specific denominational doctrine.

> [Rom. 12:4-5] (4) Just as each of us has one body with many members, and these members do not all have the same function, (5) so in Christ we who are many form one body, and each member belongs to all the others.

- We need the reliable outcome which can be widely approved by every other denomination. So we'd better entrust the theology professors who are special on this area with this task.

3. There are three types of radical spiritualism in historical point of view.

• By using Ecclesiastical distinction method, we can classify the radical spiritualism into three types; Radical syncretic spiritualism, radical renewal spiritualism and radical secessional spiritualism.

• A suspicious group or person may be involved in one or more than one types of these three. We need, first of all, to instruct the person with the warmful sound teaching of evangelical truth before we impetuously condemn him as heresy.

[James 5:19-20] (19) My brothers, if one of you should wander from the truth and someone should bring him back, (20) Remember this: Whoever turns a sinner from the error of his way will save him from death and cover over a multitude of sins.

Ⅴ. Questions for the Spiritual Ministry

1. Enumerate why the modern churches have difficulties in discriminating any groups whether they are heretical or orthodox.

_____

2. Why do we need the unified institution in order for examining heresies?

_____

3. What are three types of radical spiritualism?

_____

✝ Prayers of Daily Application

1. Probably there may be some heretical groups around you. Pray for them, so they could be rescued from the pit of darkness.
2. Pray for the heavenly wisdom so that with it you are able to teach and nurture people in right way.

Radical Syncretic Spirituality

1. The character of Gnosticism that threatened the Ancient Church

• Gnosticism had much influenced on the primitive Christianity by using mythological Persian dualism. Gnosticism frequently divided all points of world-view into the dualistic order; Light and darkness, good and evil, spiritual and material, and so on.

• Gnostics tried to make all the religions in Roman Empire become one so that there would be only one strongest unified religion in the Empire.

[1 John 4:1-3] (1)Dear friends, do not believe every spirit, but test the spirits to see whether they are from God, because many false prophets have gone out into the world. (2)This is how you *can recognize the Spirit of God: Every spirit that acknowledges that Jesus Christ has come in the flesh is from God, (3) but every spirit that does not acknowledge Jesus is not from God. This is the spirit of the antichrist, which you have heard is coming and even now is already in the world.*

[Rev. 2:20] Nevertheless, I have this against you: You tolerate that woman Jezebel, who calls herself a prophetess. By her teaching she misleads my servants into sexual immorality and the eating of food sacrificed to idols.

2. Radical syncretic spirituality which is similar to Gnosticism

• They try to mix the Christian faith with other spirituality or conviction so that they could see the one most powerful spiritual group.

• They often complain about Christian doctrine, saying that is too much irrational.

[Col. 2:8] See to it that no one takes you captive through hollow and deceptive philosophy, which depends on human tradition and the basic principles of this world rather than on Christ.

- They reenter the shamanic or magical elements in their worship or prayer style, for they regard Christian rituals as a dry emptiness.
- Neo-Gnosticism

3. Examples of the radical syncretic spiritualities

- The late Seon-Myeong Moon was the representative person of Unification Church. Moon maintained Jesus will come again in Korea, and after that, all humankind will constitute the one huge-sized of household. He had also persisted the ideal of the unification of all religions.
- There may be some suspicious groups around us of which teachings are not biblical. They are the dangerous heresies, trying to syncretize the Christian faith with the philosophical, scientific or other religious.

> [2 Peter 3:16-17] (16)He writes the same way in all his letters, speaking in them of these matters. His letters contain some things that are hard to understand, which ignorant and unstable people distort, as they do the other Scriptures, to their own destruction. (17)Therefore, dear friends, since you already know this, be on your guard so that you may not be carried away by the error of lawless men and fall from your secure position.

Questions for the Spiritual Ministry

1. Explain the motive and the character of Gnosticism.

_____

2. What is Neo-Gnosticism?

_____

3. Probably there would be some groups or churches like Neo-Gnosticism around you. Describe their syncretic attributes.

_____

† Prayers of Daily Application

1. Be alert and pray for yourself not falling to the radical syncretic spirituality.

2. Ask God for the spiritual guidance, so you can be used as God's tool for delivering people from the radical syncretic groups.

Radical Renewal Spirituality

1. The character of Montanism that threatened the Ancient Church

• Montanists very much emphasized on the advent of Holy Spirit within human soul. They believed the genuine believers receive new prophecy which exceedingly transcend the contents of the Bible.

• Montanists strictly practiced the asceticism in order that they prepared themselves for the approaching end and for the purified life.

• Montanists tried to consist the only pure church which would be spiritually innocent.

• Montanists proclaimed Jesus is coming soon, however, their activity become the model case of the radical eschatology in the primitive Christian church history.

• Montanism was rejected as heresy at 200 A.D. by main-line church through the result of several councils.

> [1 Cor. 1:10] I appeal to you, brothers, in the name of our Lord Jesus Christ, that all of you agree with one another so that there may be no divisions among you and that you may be perfectly united in mind and thought.

2. Radical renewal spirituality which is similar to Montanism

• Neo-Montanism has taken place throughout the church history whenever the church need to be renewed again.

• An effort for the church renewal will be good, if it is done according to the order of biblical ecclesiology. Therefore the renewal spirituality must go along with the spirit of unity and love of the body of Christ. Otherwise, when it is done without such spirit, it may go astray, hurting the unity of the Church.

> [1 Cor. 1:12-13] (12) What I mean is this: One of you says, "I follow Paul"; another, "I follow Apollos"; another, "I follow Cephas"; still another, "I follow Christ." (13) Is Christ divided? Was Paul crucified for you? Were you baptized into the name of Paul?

3. Examples of the radical renewal spiritualities

• Seventh Day Adventists of which founder William Miller got the false revelation that Jesus would come again in 1844.

[Matt. 24:36-37] (36) No one knows about that day or hour, not even the angels in heaven, nor the Son, but only the Father. (37) As it was in the days of Noah, so it will be at the coming of the Son of Man.

• Ellen G. White, the follower of Miller, succeeded his false teaching.

Ⅳ. Questions for the Spiritual Ministry

1. Enumerate the characters of Montanism.

_____

2. Describe the attributes of Neo-Montanism.

_____

3. What do the radical church renovators always need to be cautious about?

_____

✝ Prayers of Daily Application

1. Make every effort to work for the biblical renewal of the Church you are belong to.

2. Take the spirit of humility and self-control so that you will not disturb the order and unity of the Church.

04

Radical schismatic Spirituality

1. The character of Donatism that threatened the Ancient Church

• Donatists insisted that their community was the only authentic church, for their members seemed be all pure. They rejected the clergymen who once hid themselves from persecution before, declaring that they were not qualified as the proper persons who took charge of church.

• However, Augustine the spokesperson of the mainline church refuted the Donatists, saying they were rather heretical. Augustine condemned them as the heresy which had divided the body of Christ by their arrogancy and lack of love, declaring that the true church itself has the unity of faith and love.

[1 Cor. 12:25] so that there should be no division in the body, but that its parts should have equal concern for each other.

2. Radical separative spirituality which is similar to Donatism

• They place too much confidence in their religious legitimacy that they have no room for the spirit of unity.

[1 Cor. 1:11-13] (11) My brothers, some from Chloe's household have informed me that there are quarrels among you. (12) What I mean is this: One of you says, "I follow Paul"; another, "I follow Apollos"; another, "I follow Cephas"; still another, "I follow Christ." (13) Is Christ divided? Was Paul crucified for you? Were you baptized into the name of Paul?

• There is a difference between the church of heaven and of on the earth. The church on the earth has still been the community of pilgrim until she enters the Kingdom of Heaven. The members of the church are yet the community of sinners, although the church is the holy body of Christ.

3. Examples of the radical separative spiritualities

- Charles Taze Russel, the founder of Jehovah's Witness
- Neo-Donatism

[1 Cor. 12:27] Now you are the body of Christ, and each one of you is a part of it.

ꝰ. Questions for the Spiritual Ministry

1. What necessary conviction did the Donatists overlook in their movement?

_____

2. Explain the attribute of the radical separative spirituality.

_____

3. Do you know any groups or churches that bear resemblance to Neo-Donatism?

_____

✝ Prayers of Daily Application

1. Let the Holy Spirit search your heart whether there may be some schismatic attitude in it. If so, ask God's help for you to repent of that.

2. Be cautious of those who have the radical schismatic ecclesiology. Educate and Train people so that they may not fall into the schismatic heresies.

NOTE

NOTE

Lesson 10

Streams of the Protestant Spiritual Movement

Calvin's Pneumatology

1. Inner witness of the Holy Spirit

• John Calvin discussed about the inner witness of Holy Spirit. In his teaching, inner witness is the contrary expression to outer witness which is the sermon as written Word. When Calvin said God spoke to us through the Bible, he didn't say that we could understand what the Bible said without the ministry of Holy Spirit.

> [1 Cor. 12:13] For we were all baptized by one Spirit into one body--whether Jews or Greeks, slave or free--and we were all given the one Spirit to drink.

• Calvin thought the witness of Holy Spirit was much stronger faith than Papal Infallibility or apostolic succession of Roman

Catholicism, and exceedingly surpassed the witness of human reason. Likewise, the motive of inner witness of the Holy Spirit has been the continuing inheritance for the protestant spiritual movement, since Calvin strongly stressed its importance as the foundation and signs of the real faith.

> *[1 Cor. 2:12] We have not received the spirit of the world but the Spirit who is from God, that we may understand what God has freely given us.*

2. Union with Christ

• Union with Christ is another important means for matured spiritual life. Through that, we shall become participants of the life of Spirit. Only by faith, we can join in this kind of union. This simply means that human nature does not perform any function for this union.

• Motive that can raise the Union with Christ does not come from human effort but from the Spirit Himself. Sanctification is manifested by believer's union with Christ, and the Holy Spirit strengthens them, pursuing the way of holiness. By faith, we meet Christ and join in the Body of Christ. As soon as we join in Him, Christ comes into our heart as the mediative ministry of Holy Spirit. After that, Christians are to live with His Spirit.

[John 14:26] But the Counselor, the Holy Spirit, whom the Father will send in my name, will teach you all things and will remind you of everything I have said to you.

3. Sanctifying power of the Holy Spirit

• Regeneration has two dimensions. One is suppression against old being, and the other is participation into new being. Both dimensions aim at revival for the Imago Dei as the ultimate goal of regeneration. But this does not mean that we, in the past, who were sinners are transformed into the holy men at once. Though having been sanctified, we are not yet an actually sanctified people. Therefore, Calvin maintained that it might be recognized that sanctification was far from the practical righteousness.

• We can enjoy the conviction of victory when we are united with Christ, though we still remain in this sinful world and cannot complete our ultimate holiness. God justifies and revives His chosen people and strengthens them with His power. The gift of predestination given by the Lord is irresistible and contains the grace of endurance, in which we can overcome the temptation of sin and go forward to the holy way. Then, it could be called as the sanctifying power of Holy Spirit.

[Rom. 6:4-5] (4) We were therefore buried with him through baptism into death in order that, just as Christ was raised from the dead through the glory of the Father, we too may live a new life. (5) If we have been united with him like this in his death, we will certainly also be united with him in his resurrection.

Questions for the Spiritual Ministry

1. Describe the background why did John Calvin emphasize the idea of Inner Witness of the Holy Spirit?

_____

2. When and how the grace of Union with Christ take place in human life?

_____

3. How does the Holy Spirit work as the sanctifying power in believer's heart?

_____

✝ Prayers of Daily Application

1. Keep the full assurance of salvation in you, and live and work in accordance with the bold spirit that God gives you.

2. Yield yourself to God always so that the sanctifying power of Holy Spirit will purify you through and through.

Puritan Pneumatology

1. Holy Spirit and the witness of human conscience

• Puritans were the real expositors on human conscience.

• The conscience usually speaks to us without any relation with the will, and more over, sometimes contrary to the will. Conscience always speaks to us with its absolute authority.

• The doctrine of justification is the practical guide for human conscience. With the work of Holy Spirit, conscience instructs us the way of obeying God. Both the Holy Spirit and the conscience are rejected or submitted by us just as "the Spirit himself testifies with our spirit that we are God's children"(Rom. 8:16). This verse says that two witnesses testify our childrenship of God. Namely, the Holy Spirit confirms the witness of our conscience. Holy Spirit witnesses us the everlasting love of God no more indirectly but directly and intuitionally.

> [Rom. 8:16] The Spirit himself testifies with our spirit that we are God's children.

2. Holy Spirit and the witness of the Bible

- Men can be instructed in the meaning of Scriptural words and be made proficient in its logic, but in order that, they must be instructed by the Spirit.
- Faith originates in the result of spiritual illumination. Holy Spirit illuminates the soul, by which men can receive the spiritual things and are deeply impressed.

> [1 Cor. 2:10-12] (10) but God has revealed it to us by his Spirit. The Spirit searches all things, even the deep things of God. (11) For who among men knows the thoughts of a man except the man's spirit within him? In the same way no one knows the thoughts of God except the Spirit of God. (12) We have not received the spirit of the world but the Spirit who is from God, that we may understand what God has freely given us.

3. Assurance of salvation

• The Puritans believed that really regenerated person have some kind of signs in their souls.

• While justification brings forth the sanctification, sanctification is the witness of justification.

• Puritans often identified this conviction with the fruit of faith or characteristics of faith.

[John 1:12-13] (12) Yet to all who received him, to those who believed in his name, he gave the right to become children of God- (13) children born not of natural descent, nor of human decision or a husband's will, but born of God.

• Puritans believed that the simplest answer to the real conviction of salvation was replying positively to the question, "Have you receive Christ?"

[Rom. 10:9-10] (9) That if you confess with your mouth, "Jesus is Lord," and believe in your heart that God raised him from the dead, you will be saved. (10) For it is with your heart that you believe and are justified, and it is with your mouth that you confess and are saved.

❦ Questions for the Spiritual Ministry

1. How does the human conscience work along with the Holy Spirit in heart?

___

2. Describe the right relationship between justification and sanctification in Puritan way of thought.

___

3. Do you have an assurance of salvation? If yes, can you confess it with your mouth?

___

✝ *Prayers of Daily Application*

1. Let your conscience always be clean by the sanctifying work of Holy Spirit, and try to be guided by the Holy Spirit through the good conscience.

2. Examine your heart whether you are in the solid conviction of salvation.

Wesley's Spiritual Movement

1. Christian Perfection

• John Wesley's pneumatology is significant as we deal with the contemporary Christian pneumatology.

• The experience of Aldersgate Street at May 24, 1738

• What is the Christian Perfection? He did not teach the sinless perfection. He did not mean the perfection from the possibilities of ignorance, fault, error and even temptation.

• Sin is the intentional exercise itself. Then, his perfection teaching can be called rather a perfection in motive and in desire.

• Sinless perfection can come only after death. Until then, sanctified person will be able to live a victorious life in his continual exercise of piety.

[Matt. 5:48] Be perfect, therefore, as your heavenly Father is perfect.

2. The Second Blessing

• Two separate phases of salvation exist for the believer; One is conversion or regeneration, the other is Christian Perfection or sanctification.

[1 Thess. 5:23-24] (23)May God himself, the God of peace, sanctify you through and through. May your whole spirit, soul and body be kept blameless at the coming of our Lord Jesus Christ. (24) The one who calls you is faithful and he will do it.

• The former experience gives forgiveness for sins to believers. But the inherited sin still exists in human nature. However, by the grace of sanctification, the Second Blessing, believers are purified from the sin.

3. Instantaneous sanctification

• There are two aspects, gradual and instantaneous aspect, in Wesley's theory of sanctification, and the stress of which is instantaneous aspect. Christian perfection is given instantaneously by grace, but the continual growth also be still needed in spiritual life.

• Wesley's doctrine of entire sanctification is constituted by dual views about sin.

• In regeneration, we receive forgiveness from actual sins, but in sanctification, we are cleansed from the corruption of original sin.

[Rom. 12:1] Therefore, I urge you, brothers, in view of God's mercy, to offer your bodies as living sacrifices, holy and pleasing to God--this is your spiritual act of worship.

• You can be pured from the inherited sin by this instantaneous experience, and this motive power makes you to live victorious lives.

Questions for the Spiritual Ministry

1. How do you understand the Christian Perfection that John Wesley said?

_____

2. How did John Wesley explain the two phases of salvation?

_____

3. Contrast the instantaneous sanctification with continual growth according to the Wesleyan way of teaching.

_____

† *Prayers of Daily Application*

1. Dedicate your whole things, especially including yourself, as a living sacrifice unto the Lord.

2. Pray that you will remain in the continuous grace of entire sanctification.

Spiritual Movement of the 19th Century United States

1. **Pneumatology had been a rising contemporary issue by the 19th century in the States.**

• Some transcendental beliefs took place in the 19th century America.

• American Civil War(1861-65) had its origin in the factious issue of slavery, especially the extension of slavery into the western territories. The war had much influenced on the way of Christian belief.

• The rise and growth of interest in the doctrine of the Holy Spirit

[Acts 6:7-8] (7)So the word of God spread. The number of disciples in Jerusalem increased rapidly, and a large number of priests became obedient to the faith. (8)Now Stephen, a man full *of God's grace and power, did great wonders and miraculous signs among the people.*

2. Spiritual movement before Civil War

• There arose an interdenominational quest for holiness

[2 Cor. 7:1] Since we have these promises, dear friends, let us purify ourselves from everything that contaminates body and spirit, perfecting holiness out of reverence for God.

• Interest in the areas of evangelism and of social reform

[Matt. 5:13-16] (13) "You are the salt of the earth. But if the salt loses its saltiness, how can it be made salty again? It is no longer good for anything, except to be thrown out and trampled by men." (14) "You are the light of the world. A city on a hill cannot be hidden. (15) Neither do people light a lamp and put it under a bowl. Instead they put it on its stand, and it gives light to everyone in the house. (16) In the same way, let your light shine before men, that they may see your good deeds and praise your Father in heaven."

• Optimism or perfectionism that placed great confidence in human agency

> [Matt. 5:48] Be perfect, therefore, as your heavenly Father is perfect.

• Both Oberlin Perfectionism and Wesleyan Perfectionism explained how Christ prepared the means of grace for holiness, and taught that Christian might apply the means effectively.

3. Spiritual movement after Civil War

• American Protestantism was exceedingly confused by Higher Criticism and Darwinism that were moved from the Continent.

• Premillenarianism had much affected American Christianity and given the pessimistic view of the world. The Premillenarianism also highlighted the concern about world mission with the imminent eschatological messages.

> [Acts 1:8] But you will receive power when the Holy Spirit comes on you; and you will be my witnesses in Jerusalem, and in all Judea and Samaria, and to the ends of the earth.

• The belief that there would be a grand outpouring of the Holy Spirit just before the Second Coming of Christ

[Joel 2:28-29] (28)And afterward, I will pour out my Spirit on all people. Your sons and daughters will prophesy, your old men will dream dreams, your young men will see visions. (29)Even on my servants, both men and women, I will pour out my Spirit in those days.

• Great concern about the power of Holy Spirit with the pessimistic view of man was widely spread. So the expressions of *power of the Holy Spirit, empowering, clothed and empowered* were frequently used.

[Luke 24:48-49] (48)You are witnesses of these things. (49)I am going to send you what my Father has promised; but stay in the city until you have been clothed with power from on high.

❧ Questions for the Spiritual Ministry

1. What were two significant aspects of pre-Civil War America that had a direct relationship to the later emphasis on the doctrine of the Holy Spirit?

_____

2. What contents did both Oberlin Perfectionism and Wesleyan Perfectionism focus on?

_____

3. Describe the prominent significance of spiritual movement after Civil War in America contrasting with that of before Civil War.

_____

† *Prayers of Daily Application*

1. Pray to be worn by the purifying power of Holy Spirit in your life and ministry.

2. Pray for your effectual ministry that you will abide in the grace of the enduement of Holy Spirit.

Modern Charismatic Christianity

1. Classical Pentecostalism

• Twentieth-century Charismatic Christianity; the classical Pentecostalism, Church Renewal and the Third Wave
• Charles F. Parham, a supply pastor of the Methodist Episcopal Church, began to receive more radical issue of holiness movement.
• The Third Blessing
• Physical healing by faith

[James 5:14-16] (14)Is any one of you sick? He should call the elders of the church to pray over him and anoint him with oil in the name of the Lord. (15)And the prayer offered in faith will make the sick person well; the Lord will raise him up. If he has sinned, he will be forgiven. (16)Therefore confess your sins to each other *and pray for each other so that you may be healed. The prayer of a righteous man is powerful and effective.*

- Parham brought worldwide expansion of Pentecostal faith which directly connected speaking in other tongues with Spirit Baptism.
- The rise of Classical Pentecostalism
- Wesleyan Pentecostals and Reformed Pentecostals

[Acts 1:4-5] (4) On one occasion, while he was eating with them, he gave them this command: "Do not leave Jerusalem, but wait for the gift my Father promised, which you have heard me speak about. (5) For John baptized with water, but in a few days you will be baptized with the Holy Spirit."

[1 Cor. 14:18-19] (18) I thank God that I speak in tongues more than all of you. (19) But in the church I would rather speak five intelligible words to instruct others than ten thousand words in a tongue.

2. Charismatic Renewal

- Concerning the experience of Spirit Baptism, unlike the Pentecostals, most of Charismatics don't stress the initiative utterance of glossolalia. Rather, they more stress the importance of miracles and wonders and power encounter than glossolalia. They regard glossolalia as one of the gifts of Holy Spirit that serves for the spiritual ministry and effective prayer.

> [1 Cor. 12:28-31] (28) And in the church God has appointed first of all apostles, second prophets, third teachers, then workers of miracles, also those having gifts of healing, those able to help others, those with gifts of administration, and those speaking in different kinds of tongues. (29) Are all apostles? Are all prophets? Are all teachers? Do all work miracles? (30) Do all have gifts of healing? Do all speak in tongues? Do all interpret? (31) But eagerly desire the greater gifts. And now I will show you the most excellent way.

• Charismatics seem weaker than Classical Pentecostalism in their missionary motivation. They prefer to invite Christians to the experience of Holy Spirit rather than to go toward the gentiles and unbelievers.

• Charismatic renewal had made most progress in the white-middle class people of society rather than in black and lower class.

• Charismatic Renewal Movement has been widely spreaded in the churches of the world, especially in Asia.

3. the Third Wave

- John Wimber and Vineyard Theology
- The different character of the Third Wave from the Classical Pentecostalism and from the Charismatic Renewal
- What does the Baptism with the Holy Spirit mean in viewpoint of the Third Wavers? They mostly considered Spirit Baptism as the another aspect of regeneration, or as the ongoing experience of being filled with the Holy Spirit.

> *[1 Cor. 12:13] For we were all baptized by one Spirit into one body--whether Jews or Greeks, slave or free--and we were all given the one Spirit to drink.*

- Peter Wagner and the New Apostolic Reformation
- Wagner's teaching on Five-fold official duties

> *[Eph. 4;11] It was he who gave some to be apostles, some to be prophets, some to be evangelists, and some to be pastors and teachers.*

- Many of them did not accent the speaking in other tongues as the accurate sign of receiving Spirit Baptism.
- George Eldon Ladd at Fuller Theological Seminary interpreted the Kingdom of God as the real presence of God's power which

overcome the Satanic power.

[Matt. 12:28] But if I drive out demons by the Spirit of God, then the kingdom of God has come upon you.

❧ Questions for the Spiritual Ministry

1. Enumerate the representative three charismatic movements of the twentieth century.

_____

2. What spiritual manifestation does the Classical Pentecostalism focus on?

_____

3. Differentiate the character of the Third Wave from that of other two, i.e., Classical Pentecostalism and the Charismatic Renewal.

_____

✝ Prayers of Daily Application

1. You will need greater and more abundant fruits for serving God. Pray for being baptized with the Holy Spirit.

2. If you are a person who are speaking in other tongues, practice it more today with the sincere heart to God.

NOTE

NOTE

Lesson 11

Holy Spirit and the Communities

Communities of New Birth

***1.* Holy Spirit works for the new birth of sinners in the communities.**

• We need to pray that all the members of the community should repent and receive Jesus Christ as Lord.

[1 Peter 1:23] For you have been born again, not of perishable seed, but of imperishable, through the living and enduring word of God.

• Only regenerated persons can understand and practice God's will for the expansion of Kingdom of Heaven on earth.

• The life of Jesus in us is the real holy seed for the expansion of Kingdom of God in our communities.

2. Holy Spirit leads the communities into the life of confession and forgiveness of sins.

• There still remain the sinful depravity in our souls that makes many troubles not just only in us but also in the communities.

• Holy Spirit awakens our conscience so that we must repent and forsake the attitude and behavior of sinful desires.

> [James 5:16] Therefore confess your sins to each other and pray for each other so that you may be healed. The prayer of a righteous man is powerful and effective.

• We have to confess and forgive our sins each other.

3. Holy Spirit guides the communities to the sanctified life in Christ.

• In community life, we are too much inclined to the selfish and sinful desires rather than God's will.

> [1 Cor. 3:1-3] (1)Brothers, I could not address you as spiritual but as worldly--mere infants in Christ. (2)I gave you milk, not solid food, for you were not yet ready for it. Indeed, you are still not ready. (3) You are still worldly. For since there is jealousy and quarreling among you, are you not worldly? Are you not acting like mere men?

- Self-denial and suppression of sins should be required in the community life to be sanctified.
- The process of sanctification has dual functions; One is the power of crucifixion that weakens and kills the old nature, and the other is the power of resurrection that strengthens and revives the new nature.

☙ Questions for the Spiritual Ministry

1. Why do we have to pray and work for the new birth of sinners in our community?

_____

2. As for the sinfulness in the community members, what does the Holy Spirit want to do for their harmony and spiritual growth?

_____

3. What are the dual functions of Holy Spirit for the holiness of the community we belong to?

_____

✝ Prayers of Daily Application

1. Pray for the repentance and regeneration of community members.

2. Pray that your community will grow in Christ through the grace of sanctification.

02

Communities of Healing and Restoration

***1*. Holy Spirit heals the physical disease among community members.**

• When someone is sick in bed, what should we do first for him or for her?

[Mal. 4:2] But for you who revere my name, the sun of righteousness will rise with healing in its wings. And you will go out and leap like calves released from the stall.

• Seek the Lord's will.
• Without medicine, only with prayer?

2. Holy Spirit delivers the communities from the influence of the demons.

- Demonic forces around us

[James 4:7] Submit yourselves, then, to God. Resist the devil, and he will flee from you.

- What do demons do in the communities?

[Mark 16:17] And these signs will accompany those who believe: In my name they will drive out demons; they will speak in new tongues.

- Perform the power of deliverance or of casting out demons.

3. Holy Spirit guides the communities to the process of inner healing.

- The process of holiness in the communities
- Anxiety, sense of inferiority, indignation, jealousy, hatred and guilty sense
- Repentance of inner sinfulness

[Rev. 3:19] Those whom I love I rebuke and discipline. So be

earnest, and repent.

Questions for the Spiritual Ministry

1. Do we have a privilege to pray for the sick to be healed?

_____

2. Do you have any experience to cast demons out of others? If yes, share with us.

_____

3. When you meet those who desperately need their own inner healing, what should you do for them?

_____

† Prayers of Daily Application

1. Pray for the community members who are suffering from disease so that they could be cured.
2. Cast demons out of the community life through the guidance and power of Holy Spirit.

Communities being guided by the Holy Spirit

1. **Holy Spirit wants to dwell with the community members and to make close intimacy with them.**

• Christian community is the spiritual organization of which head is Jesus Christ.

• How can we properly discern God's will in the community?

[Exodus 40:36-37] (36)In all the travels of the Israelites, whenever the cloud lifted from above the tabernacle, they would set out; (37) but if the cloud did not lift, they did not set out--until the day it lifted.

• Everyday spiritual discipline must be practiced for the better Christian community.

2. Holy Spirit guides the communities to the way of victorious life overcoming all temptations.

• We can experience the overcoming Christian life, if we are faithfully guided by the Holy Spirit.

[Gal. 5:16] So I say, live by the Spirit, and you will not gratify the desires of the sinful nature.

• This does not mean that we never face with the temptations until we die.
• All the members of community have to sincerely follow Spiritual guidance so that they can triumph over the sins in their community life.

[Gal. 5:18] But if you are led by the Spirit, you are not under law.

3. Holy Spirit wants to bear the fruit of God's will in our community life.

• How should we dedicate ourselves in order to bear good fruits for the glory of God?
• Talk and pray about God's will in everything with each other.

[Matt. 18:19-20] (19) Again, I tell you that if two of you on earth

agree about anything you ask for, it will be done for you by my Father in heaven. (20)For where two or three come together in my name, there am I with them.

- To become better spiritual community, we need more dedication and intimate sharing among members.

ℓ. Questions for the Spiritual Ministry

1. How do we make our community life have close intimacy with the Holy Spirit?

_____

2. There might be many kinds of temptation in our community life. How can the community members defeat the temptations relying on the Holy Spirit?

_____

3. Have you found out the will of God for your community? Talk each other about it.

_____

✝ *Prayers of Daily Application*

1. Pray that your community members will have closer intimacy with the Holy Spirit more day after day.

2. Pray that your community will be overflown with the victorious testimonies which triumph over all the temptations.

Communities of Full Dedication

***1.* Holy Spirit makes the community members confess the death of old being through the confession of Union with Christ.**

• The truth Union with Christ is the necessary condition for the better spiritual community.

[Gal. 5:24] *Those who belong to Christ Jesus have crucified the sinful nature with its passions and desires.*

• Holy Spirit makes the band of unity.
• Practical use of identification of crucifixion

2. Holy Spirit guides the communities to the life wholly dedicated to the Lord.

• Why does the full dedication of every member is necessary in the communities?

> [Matt. 16:24] Then Jesus said to his disciples, "If anyone would come after me, he must deny himself and take up his cross and follow me."

• Full dedication will need the steady resolution of our free will.
• Firm evangelical attitude; dying with Jesus, living with Jesus

3. Holy Spirit uses the communities as the tool for the fulfillment of God's evangelization for the world.

• The noble mission of Christian communities

> [Isaiah 61:1-3] (1)The Spirit of the Sovereign LORD is on me, because the LORD has anointed me to preach good news to the poor. He has sent me to bind up the brokenhearted, to proclaim freedom for the captives and release from darkness for the prisoners, (2)to proclaim the year of the LORD'S favor and the day of vengeance of our God, to comfort all who mourn, (3)and provide for those who grieve in Zion--to bestow on them a crown

of beauty instead of ashes, the oil of gladness instead of mourning, and a garment of praise instead of a spirit of despair. They will be called oaks of righteousness, a planting of the LORD for the display of his splendor.

• Growing in the conviction of twofold vision; Christlikeness and World evangelization

Questions for the Spiritual Ministry

1. Do you know the truth of crucifixion with Jesus? Share it with other members.

_____

2. What kinds of practice do we need in our community for the fully dedicated life unto the Lord?

_____

3. Why has God used your community in His hand up to date? What will be God's ultimate vision for your community?

_____

✝ Prayers of Daily Application

1. Share the truth with your community that your old being has been crucified with Christ Jesus.

2. Pray that all the members of your community will dedicate their lives to God for God's glory.

05

Communities of the Lordship of Holy Spirit

1. Holy Spirit leads the communities into the life that walk with Him wholeheartedly.

[Eph. 4:15-16] (15)Instead, speaking the truth in love, we will in all things grow up into him who is the Head, that is, Christ. (16)From him the whole body, joined and held together by every supporting ligament, grows and builds itself up in love, as each part does its work.

• God wants all the members of community can walk with the Holy Spirit.

2. Holy Spirit sanctifies the communities up to the full measure of love of Christlikeness.

- How can we bear Christlike fruits in the communities?
- Love for God, love for others

[Matt. 12:29-31] (29) "The most important one," answered Jesus, "is this: 'Hear, O Israel, the Lord our God, the Lord is one. (30) Love the Lord your God with all your heart and with all your soul and with all your mind and with all your strength.' (31) The second is this: 'Love your neighbor as yourself.' There is no commandment greater than these."

- Love for God is not just only a foundation of personal holiness but also of social holiness.

3. Holy Spirit makes the communities proclaim gospel with spiritual power.

[Matt. 24:14] And this gospel of the kingdom will be preached in the whole world as a testimony to all nations, and then the end will come.

- The community well-equipped by the lifestyle of the Lordship of Holy Spirit is the community of powerful evangelization.

❦ Questions for the Spiritual Ministry

1. Practice and set examples for the life walking with the Holy Spirit in your community life.

___

2. Pray for each other so that they would grow up to the full measure of Christlikeness.

___

3. Make vision for your community so that it would become a powerful troops of God for evangelism.

___

† *Prayers of Daily Application*

1. Pray that your community life will be characterized by Spirit-filled lifestyle, having close intimacy with the Holy Spirit at all times.

2. Pray that your community will bear much fruits to proclaim the gospel.

NOTE

NOTE

Lesson 12

The Lordship of Holy Spirit

Developmental Course of the Pneumatology

1. Modern Wesleyan holiness movement

• Modern Wesleyan holiness movement shows its preservation of the motive of purity and power and the attitude of tolerance upon the spiritual gifts.

> [Ezekiel 36:25-27] (25)I will sprinkle clean water on you, and you will be clean; I will cleanse you from all your impurities and from all your idols. (26)I will give you a new heart and put a new spirit in you; I will remove from you your heart of stone and give you a heart of flesh. (27)And I will put my Spirit in you and move you to follow my decrees and be careful to keep my laws.

• There also be seen the effort that Wesleyan ministers are trying to deal the understanding of the Holy Spirit with Christology.

2. Reformed Pneumatology

• It shows its preservation of the motive of Union with Christ as the core point of Reformed Pneumatology. There have been a tendency that the use of speaking in other tongues and divine healing, and that the application of signs and wonders.

> [1 Cor. 12:12-13] (12) The body is a unit, though it is made up of many parts; and though all its parts are many, they form one body. So it is with Christ. (13) For we were all baptized by one Spirit into one body--whether Jews or Greeks, slave or free--and we were all given the one Spirit to drink.

3. Pentecostal spiritual movement

• Many Pentecostals nowaday say that Speaking in other tongues is nothing more than the one of the spiritual gifts rather than the sign of Spirit Baptism.
• Supplement of the motive of Union with Christ and Purity.

> [Acts 19:4-7] (4) Paul said, "John's baptism was a baptism of repentance. He told the people to believe in the one coming after

him, that is, in Jesus." (5) On hearing this, they were baptized into the name of the Lord Jesus. (6) When Paul placed his hands on them, the Holy Spirit came on them, and they spoke in tongues and prophesied. (7) There were about twelve men in all.

• More frequent use of term Fullness of the Holy Spirit rather than Baptism with the Holy Spirit

[Eph. 5:18] Do not get drunk on wine, which leads to debauchery. Instead, be filled with the Spirit.

Questions for the Spiritual Ministry

1. What tendencies does the modern Wesleyan holiness movement have nowaday?

_____

2. Why does the recent Reformed Pneumatology show tendency that welcome the spiritual gifts or signs and wonders?

_____

3. Is there any change of conviction in Pentecostal spiritual movement in terms of speaking in other tongues nowaday comparing with that of past days?

✝ Prayers of Daily Application

1. Make every effort to have closer intimacy with the Holy Spirit who is the Spirit of Christ Jesus.

2. Ask the Lord that He will bestow the heavenly power and manifestation upon your ministry.

Holistic Pneumatology

1. What is Holistic Pneumatology?

• Holistic Pneumatology is the synthetic theory of the Holy Spirit which interchanges and supplements the good points among the various pneumatologies.

• What does the Holistic Pneumatology aim for? The emphasis on the Union with Christ and the power of evangelism accompanying with spiritual gifts is the general phenomena in every types of pneumatology.

[1 Cor. 2:4-5] (4)My message and my preaching were not with wise and persuasive words, but with a demonstration of the Spirit's power, (5)so that your faith might not rest on men's wisdom, but on God's power.

2. Holistic Pneumatology aims at Christlikeness.

• The one of the pair axes of Holistic Pneumatology is the motive of Union with Christ.

• The motive of Union with Christ apparently aims at Christlikeness which is the embodiment of the image of God.

> [Eph. 4:15-16] (15) Instead, speaking the truth in love, we will in all things grow up into him who is the Head, that is, Christ. (16) From him the whole body, joined and held together by every supporting ligament, grows and builds itself up in love, as each part does its work.

3. Holistic Pneumatology maintains the power of evangelism.

• Another axis of Holistic Pneumatology is the emphasis upon the power of Holy Spirit that accompanies the spiritual gifts.

> [1 Cor. 14:39] Therefore, my brothers, be eager to prophesy, and do not forbid speaking in tongues.

> [Acts 20:22-24] (22) And now, compelled by the Spirit, I am going to Jerusalem, not knowing what will happen to me there. (23) I only know that in every city the Holy Spirit warns me that prison and hardships are facing me. (24) However, I consider my life worth

nothing to me, if only I may finish the race and complete the task the Lord Jesus has given me--the task of testifying to the gospel of God's grace.

Questions for the Spiritual Ministry

1. What is Holistic Pneumatology?

_____

2. Explain the relationship between Union with Christ and Christlikeness in terms of Holistic Pneumatology.

_____

3. What are two major axes of Holistic Pneumatology?

_____

† Prayers of Daily Application

1. Have you ever grieved the Holy Spirit because of your sinful desires or vain conceits? If so, repent of that.

2. Is there any guilt in you which does not follow Spiritual guidance? If there is, repent your sins to God and be purified.

Definition of the Lordship of Holy Spirit

1. The core of Holistic Pneumatology is the Lordship of Holy Spirit.

• The power of purity, power for service, and the spiritual gifts may be manifested as you receive the power of Holy Spirit. But the most important phenomenon of which is the life that realizes the Lordship of Holy Spirit.

• What's the meaning of the Lordship of Holy Spirit? It is the work that Jesus Christ who is the chief of the Christian life and evangelism guides personally in every believer as the person of Holy Spirit.

[Col. 1:26-29] (26) the mystery that has been kept hidden for ages and generations, but is now disclosed to the saints. (27) To them

God has chosen to make known among the Gentiles the glorious riches of this mystery, which is Christ in you, the hope of glory. (28) We proclaim him, admonishing and teaching everyone with all wisdom, so that we may present everyone perfect in Christ. (29) To this end I labor, struggling with all his energy, which so powerfully works in me.

2. How is the Lordship of Holy Spirit manifested?

• Lordship of the Holy Spirit is realized *by the* life *that the wholly-consecrated believer witnesses Gospel with the manifestation of Holy Spirit and with the power walking with the Lord Jesus at every moment.*

[Col. 3:23] Whatever you do, work at it with all your heart, as working for the Lord, not for men.

[1 John 2:6] Whoever claims to live in him must walk as Jesus did.

3. What is the purpose of the Lordship of Holy Spirit?

• *The wholly-consecrated believer:* we can live sanctified lives that are wholly consecrated to the Lord.
• *Walking with the Lord Jesus at every moment:* we can communicate

with the Lord personally without ceasing.

• *Witnesses Gospel with the manifestation of Holy Spirit and with the power*: we can proclaim the Gospel with the supernatural power of Holy Spirit.

• *The life:* We can experience the Lordship of Holy Spirit not only in the instantaneous event but also in our daily life-style continually.

[Phil. 2:5] Your attitude should be the same as that of Christ Jesus.

Questions for the Spiritual Ministry

1. Explain the meaning of the Lordship of Holy Spirit.

___

2. How is the Lordship of Holy Spirit realized in Christian life?

___

3. Show your practical example how you walk with the Holy Spirit without ceasing.

___

† *Prayers of Daily Application*

1. Try to be aware of God's presence and to dwell in His government at all times.

2. Yield your whole intelligence, emotion and free will to God so that the Holy Spirit can rule over your life always.

Life of the Lordship of Holy Spirit

1. The Lordship of Holy Spirit goes toward the accomplishment of our sanctification.

• To receive Holy Spirit, which is the beginning of the whole lifetime process toward Christlikeness.

[John 17:21-23] (21) that all of them may be one, Father, just as you are in me and I am in you. May they also be in us so that the world may believe that you have sent me. (22) I have given them the glory that you gave me, that they may be one as we are one: (23) I in them and you in me. May they be brought to complete unity to let the world know that you sent me and have loved them even as you have loved me.

• Becoming like Christ, which is not by human efforts or merits but by the power and guidance of Holy Spirit.

[Rom. 8:9] You, however, are controlled not by the sinful nature but by the Spirit, if the Spirit of God lives in you. And if anyone does not have the Spirit of Christ, he does not belong to Christ.

2. The Lordship of Holy Spirit owns the power of evangelism.

• The power and gifts of Holy Spirit will be manifested in our life and ministry as we walk with Him in intimacy.

[1 Cor. 12:4-11] (4) There are different kinds of gifts, but the same Spirit. (5) There are different kinds of service, but the same Lord. (6) There are different kinds of working, but the same God works all of them in all men. (7) Now to each one the manifestation of the Spirit is given for the common good. (8) To one there is given through the Spirit the message of wisdom, to another the message of knowledge by means of the same Spirit, (9) to another faith by the same Spirit, to another gifts of healing by that one Spirit, (10) to another miraculous powers, to another prophecy, to another distinguishing between spirits, to another speaking in different kinds of tongues, and to still another the interpretation of tongues. (11) All

these are the work of one and the same Spirit, and he gives them to each one, just as he determines.

• The Lordship of Holy Spirit, the reign of the Spirit of Christ in us, is much more valuable than the manifestation and the fruit of Holy Spirit.

3. The believers that confess the Lordship of Holy Spirit have been found increasingly lately.

• Holistic Pneumatology that emphasizes the Union with Christ and the spiritual power of evangelism has been the general confession of the belief of Pneumatology nowaday.

[Acts 1:8] But you will receive power when the Holy Spirit comes on you; and you will be my witnesses in Jerusalem, and in all Judea and Samaria, and to the ends of the earth.

• There is a dual dimension of Spirit Baptism; The dimension of Spiritual Truth and of Experience. The former is the real source of the Lordship of Holy Spirit, while the latter is the embodiment of it.

❆ Questions for the Spiritual Ministry

1. Talk about how the Holy Spirit initiates and guides His ministry of holiness in believer's life.

_____

2. Describe how much more the Lordship of Holy Spirit is valuable than the manifestation and fruit of Holy Spirit.

_____

3. Explain the relationship between Dual dimension of Spirit Baptism and the Lordship of Holy Spirit.

_____

✝ *Prayers of Daily Application*

1. Examine yourself now whether you are in the life style of the Lordship of Holy Spirit.
2. Pray that your lifetime will be deeply involved in the Lordship of Holy Spirit as you imitate Christ and as you proclaim gospel through the power of Holy Spirit.

NOTE

NOTE

NOTE

Appendix I

The Main Points in Church History

A.D.30
Old Catholic Age

600
the Middle Age

Acts 1:8
Jerusalem - Rome
A.D.313
Development of Trinity
& Christology
Apostolic Fathers
& Apologists
Augustine

Eastern Church
 & Western Church
Emperor & Pope
Scholasticism
Mysticism
Renaissance

Greek Orthodox Church

Roman Catholic Church

Protestant Church

| 1100 | 1500 | 1600 | 2000 |

Reformation Era   **Recent & Modern Times**

Martin Luther
Zwingli, Knox & Calvin
Counter Reformation
The Council of Trent
  (1545 - 1563)

Protestant Scholasticism
Pietism & Rationalism
Methodists
Liberal Theologians
Neo Orthodoxism
Ecumenical Movement
  Three Waves
  W.C.C.
"Proclaim Christ
  Until He Comes"
1989, Manila
  Lausanne II
Oct. 2010, Cape Town
  Lausanne III

Appendix II

Rise of the Protestant Pneumatology

16 C	17 C	18 C
Calvin	**Puritans**	**Wesley**
▷ Inner Witness of HS ▷ Union with Christ ▷ sanctifying power	▷ witness of HS and human conscience ▷ witness of HS and the Bible ▷ assurance of salvation	▷ relation with the Puritan spirituality ▷ Christian Perfection ▷ Second Blessing ▷ instantaneous sanctification **Jonathan Edwards** ▷ Religious Affection

19 C	20 C
Wesleyan-Holiness Movement ▷Phoebe Palmer ▷spiritual movement after the Civil War ▷Spirit Baptism: purity and power ▷Classical Wesleyans and Radical Wesleyans ▷Fire-Baptized Holiness Church	**Pentecostalism** ▷Spirit Baptism and Speaking in Other Tongues ▷Wesleyan Pentecostalism and Reformed Pentecostalism
Reformed Spiritual Movement ▷Spirit Baptism: power for service ▷A. B. Simpson ▷Recent Reformed Spiritual Movement and Orthodox Reformed Pneumatology	**Charismatic Renewal** ▷contrast with the Classical Pentecostalism: Speaking in Other Toungues, Spirit Baptism, participation
	the Third Wave ▷Vineyard Movement ▷global expansion

Appendix III

The Power of Holy Spirit Seminar
Luke 24:49

1. Why Do We Need to Receive the Power of Holy Spirit?

• If you want to live the victorious and powerful Christian life, you need to ask God for wisdom and power that are given by the Holy Spirit. And it must be necessary especially for Christian workers that they receive the power of Holy Spirit first of all.

• Just look around your pastoral situation. How much do you need to be filled with the power of Holy Spirit?

• Text: This power originated not from man;

☞ *With power from on high(Luke 24:49)*

☞ *My message and my preaching were not with wise and persuasive words, but with a demonstration of the Spirit's power, so that your faith might not rest on men's wisdom, but on God's power(1 Cor. 2:4-5).*

2. Who is the Holy Spirit?

• Holy Spirit is the Spirit of Jesus Christ and of God. Triune God cannot be separated. Receiving Jesus and receiving the Holy Spirit are the same experience.

• Look at the harmony of the triune God;

☞ *When the <u>Counselor</u> comes, whom <u>I</u> will send to you from the Father, the Spirit of truth who goes out from the <u>Father</u>, he will* *testify about me(John 15:26).*

☞ *And <u>I</u> will ask the <u>Father</u>, and he will give you <u>another Counselor</u> to be with you forever(John 14:16).*

• When you receive Jesus Christ as your Savior and Lord, the Holy Spirit come into your heart and begins to abide in you.

• Sometimes you may be confused when you hear the various expressions concerning the fullness of Holy Spirit as follows; receive the Holy Spirit, receive the baptism with the Holy Spirit, receive the power of Holy Spirit, or be filled with the Holy Spirit, etc.

• Then, you had better understand the meaning of which like this way; It is not the meaning that the Holy Spirit does not abide in you, but the meaning that already existing Spirit gives new power for you.

3. Baptism with the Holy Spirit or the Fullness of Holy Spirit?

• There have been many confusing theological controversies about the terminology of Spirit Baptism so far, but the conflictions have not been adjusted until now;

1) The issue is concerning the time of Spirit Baptism; At the time when we are regenerated or after being regenerated?

2) Is the Spirit Baptism same with the fullness of Holy Spirit or not?

• Though various explanations may be possible according to many doctrinal situations of every denomination, some differences of explanation are shown like these in general;

1) In some Presbyterian and Baptist Churches, they generally regard Spirit Baptism occurs at the time of regeneration. And they say that there may be only continuing experiences of the fullness of Holy Spirit after regeneration.

However, there must be another spiritual position even in those denominations; Some of them clearly differentiate Spirit Baptism from regeneration, namely, which occurs when believers experience the power of Holy Spirit after their time of regeneration.

2) Pentecostals especially stress the speaking in other tongues. They regard the speaking in other tongues as the assured sign of receiving Spirit Baptism.

3) In Holiness and in Methodist Churches, they doctrinally stress the experience of purifying sinfulness which can be experienced after regeneration.

4) Recently in Charismatic Renewal or in the Third Wave, they like to use the term the fullness of Holy Spirit more than Baptism with the Holy Spirit.

• However, there are growing contemporary tendencies that the various explanations are mixed, having no concern with their denominational statements.

• One thing is very clear; No matter how much various expressions may be, Spirit Baptism is the spiritual truth that the regenerated believers are united with Jesus Christ by the mediation of the Holy Spirit. Then, on the basis of such conviction, which gives you the instantaneous powerful experience.

• Thus, dual dimensions may be possible to explain the confused doctrines of Spirit Baptism. These are the dimension of spiritual truth and of experiment. I named these as the dual dimensions of Spirit Baptism.

• We can clearly know whether we have received the experience or not.

☞ *but stay in the city until you have been clothed with power(Luke 24:49).*

• For examples, cite the testimonies of some great evangelists such as John Wesley, Billy Graham and D. L. Moody.

4. When and How We Receive the Power of Holy Spirit?

• Until when do you pray for that? The right time is when you are aware that your dedicated soul is under the control of the Holy Spirit wholly;

☞ *On one occasion, while he was eating with them, he gave them this command: "Do not leave Jerusalem, but wait for the gift my Father promised, which you have heard me speak about. For John baptized with water, but in a few days you will be baptized with the Holy Spirit"(Acts 1:4,5).*

• Waiting must be need, by which you can concretely count and decide yourself for perfect consecration to the Lord. Already prepared, you don't need to hesitate. It is yours. Because, that is the grace already prepared by God for you.

• How do you know that? And what about the following experiences? As you receive the Spirit Baptism, you may experience the physical manifestation or not. But it is not necessary thing. It is not the core of Spirit Baptism.

• The most important checking point is whether you are under the control of the Holy Spirit or not. You will know the time the power of Holy Spirit come upon you, when you are fully certain that you are under the control of the Holy Spirit.

5. What is the Result of Having Received Spirit Baptism?

• The power of purity, power for service, and the spiritual gifts may be manifested as you receive the power of Holy Spirit. But the most important phenomenon of which is the life that makes you live according to the Lordship of Holy Spirit.

• What's the meaning of the Lordship of Holy Spirit? It is the work that Jesus Christ who is the chief of the Christian life and evangelism guides personally in every believer as the person of Holy Spirit (Bonjour Bay, *The 21st Century Jesus Revival* (Seoul: Unseong, 1998, 202).

★ *'The Lordship of Holy Spirit' is realized by the life that the wholly-consecrated believer witnesses Gospel with the manifestation of*

Holy Spirit and with the power walking with the Lord Jesus at every moment.

• The Lordship of Holy Spirit means as follows;

1) *The wholly-consecrated believer:* we can live sanctified lives that are wholly consecrated to the Lord.

2) *Walking with the Lord Jesus at every moment:* we can communicate with the Lord personally without ceasing.

3) *Witnesses Gospel with the manifestation of Holy Spirit and with the power:* we can proclaim the Gospel with the supernatural power of Holy Spirit.

4) *The life:* we can experience the Lordship of Holy Spirit not only in the instantaneous event but also in our daily life-style continually.

Appendix IV

The Lordship of Holy Spirit

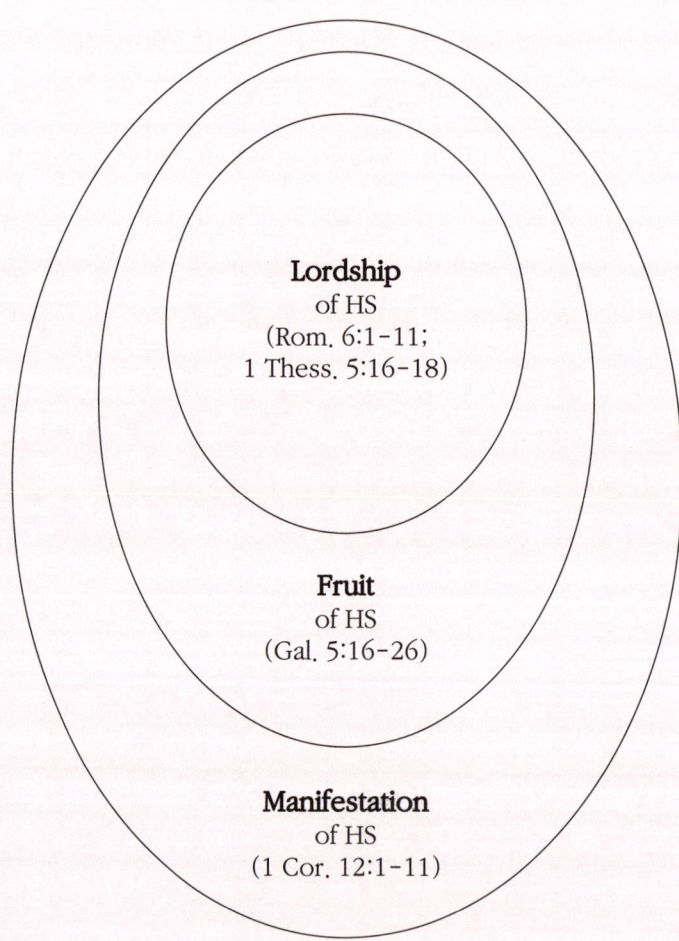

Lordship
of HS
(Rom. 6:1-11;
1 Thess. 5:16-18)

Fruit
of HS
(Gal. 5:16-26)

Manifestation
of HS
(1 Cor. 12:1-11)

Lordship of HS maintains the power of **Sanctification** in our heart.

Fruit of HS aims for the full realization of our **Christlikeness**.

Manifestation of HS works for the accomplishment of **World Evangelization**.